Afflictio

Circumcisio
Infibulation
Africa

Raqiya Haji

Dedicated to the Somali W
which has fought and strug
status of and discriminatio
aspects of their economic,

Zed Press, 57 Caledonian Road, London N1 9DN.

Sisters in Affliction was first published
by Zed Press, 57 Caledonian Road,
London N1 9DN in 1982.

Copyedited by Anna Gourlay
Proofread by Rosamund Howe
Cover design by Jan Brown
Typeset by Jo Marsh
Printed by Krips Repro, Meppel, Holland

British Library Cataloguing in Publication Data

Abdalla, Raqiya Haji Dualeh
Sisters in affliction.
1. Infibulation
I. Title
618.8 GN481

ISBN 0-86232-093-3
IBSN 0-86232-094-1 Pbk

U.S. Distributor
Lawrence Hill & Co., 520 Riverside
Avenue, Westport, Conn. 06880.

Contents

Acknowledgements

In writing the dissertation upon which this book is based I was helped by many individuals, organizations and institutions. I wish to thank my Ministry — the Ministry of Culture and Higher Education in Somalia — for allowing me to undertake this post-graduate course, especially Mrs Faduma Ahmed Alim, the Assistant Minister, who helped me to obtain the opportunity to study.

It goes without saying that I owe many thanks to the people in Somalia who helped me to carry out the interviews and to the respondents who participated.

I also express my gratitude to the many people who supported, encouraged and assisted me. In particular, I am deeply indebted to Maria Mies for her guidance and encouragement; thanks also to Kumari Jayawardena for her helpful suggestions and comments.

Without access to the documents and publications of several organizations, and to literature obtained from individuals, all of whose names I regret there is not space here to mention individually, my study would not have been possible. But I must make special mention of the World Health Organization (WHO), in particular the Regional Office for the Eastern Mediterranean in Egypt, Alexandria, for the documents and literature they placed at my disposal.

I am grateful to the library staff of the ISS who obtained books and documents I needed from outside libraries. In particular, I would like to thank Maria Jose for her special attention and concern for my requirements. Thanks too, to Jane Wild who typed my original thesis.

I am grateful to the European Economic Commission (EEC) for financing my studies at the Institute of Social Studies, The Hague.

My good friends Dana Peebles, Elias Habte Selassie, Rhoda Roddock, Shireen Samarasuria, Mary Walker and Lance Tulloch, helped me with material and moral support at all times. To them I express many thanks.

For encouraging me to come to the Netherlands to study and for her continuing support I would also like to thank Mia Berden. Last, but not least, I must thank my family; my husband especially, for his patience during my long absence.

Raqiya Haji Dualeh Abdalla

Introduction and Background

History reveals that the problem of social inequality between women and men has been the subject of contention for centuries. Many men, in opposing the progress of women, argue that the rights they have already obtained are excessive. Such attitudes indicate that the need to struggle is far from finished.

While this struggle must take place on all levels, in particular women must fight against those prejudices, out-moded concepts and ideologies of contempt that hamper their abilities and rob them of self-confidence, and have done so throughout history. To understand and to fight them effectively, an appreciation of their historical evolution is necessary, and this aspect will be stressed here, based upon factual research which aims to assess the present and potential situation of women, particularly with regard to the practice of genital mutilation of women in Somalia.

The sexual oppression of women takes different forms and is achieved by different methods, ranging from the subtle to the overt: economic, intellectual, physical and psychological. The control of women's bodies and the oppression of their sexuality, in one form or another, exists in *every society* in the world. Attitudes stemming from this same form of oppression have been responsible for many kinds of sexual assaults on women, as well as resulting in them being ignored and efforts made to ensure they are generally kept in ignorance. While men enjoy increasing freedom, women are subjected to more fear, restrictions and physical mutilation. These tendencies are notable in many different societies throughout the world. For example female genital mutilation is still practiced among many African tribes and thousands of young girls are still, today, subjected to this, Clearly this is a denial of a fundamental human right to health, the inviolability of the body and natural sexuality to a large number of people, simply because they are women.

In Somalia, the practice of genital mutilation has persisted for centuries and is still prevalent among all classes of females in both rural and urban areas. While the Somali nation has changed in many ways and the Revolution of 1969 achieved a great deal for the people in all aspects of economic, social, cultural and political life, the ancient custom of genital mutilation of women continues to be practiced. Almost no one, so far, has had the courage to speak openly about it because of the taboo attached to sexual matters.

This taboo and secrecy surrounding the continuation of this brutal practice, the unwillingness of those involved in it to face reality, and the excuse that cultural practices are sacrosanct, are no longer convincing to many Somali women today. They realize that action must be taken now, against this mutilation which humiliates and degrades them. Their former silence was not because they did not experience pain and suffering, but because they were unaware that other alternatives to silent acceptance did exist.

There is no longer any reason, given the present state of progress in science, to tolerate confusion and ignorance about reproduction and women's sexuality. They must not permit their bodies to be crippled and deliberately mutilated to serve a male-dominated ideology and interests. Mutilation of women cannot simply be seen as an accidental occurrence of a redundant tradition. Its occurrence and persistence throughout the ages in many cultures, necessitates a search for the reasons upon which it might have been based. The institutions that perpetuate the practice and the factors contributing to it must be challenged.

One of the best approaches towards a campaign to eliminate this custom is to disseminate facts, information and an understanding of the complexity of the problem from a woman's point of view. Thus, the main objective of this book is to initiate action to abandon the practice of female circumcision, especially in the Somali Democratic Republic where the more drastic forms of these operations are performed and still are not seen as a social problem, except by a very few enlightened women and men.

No change is possible without the conscious participation of women. It is our duty as women to fight to abolish this practice which is imposed on young girls by old customs and erroneous beliefs. I believe that only women themselves can create awareness in their society, influence change in society's attitudes, fight against the humiliation of this practice and urge its total abolition. This book is intended to stimulate such actions, and to involve all those — men and women — who are concerned with change and human development.

To accomplish this requires sufficient knowledge, and investigation of the problem in its various aspects. I shall attempt to correct some of the misconceptions and myths surrounding this practice, as well as to create an awareness of its health hazards. The results of my research are aimed at convincing people and government of the need to eradicate the custom, by showing them clear, factual evidence of its harmfulness to the physical and psychological well-being of women and young girls. My objective is to help bring about significant actions, including legislation, to eradicate the practice.

I have attempted here to provide a basic record of female genital mutilation, with a multi-dimensional view of the problems rather than to concentrate on one aspect of the practice. It is based on many sources: previous literature on the subject, my own experience and observations of the practice since my childhood, as well as information and statements gathered through empirical investigations involving other Somali women, interpreting their own feelings and ideas about the custom.

Whilst this does not claim to be the first published account of the practice (which dates back 2000 years), the literature on the subject is both scarce and limited in scope, and its lack of an historical and social dimension is a specific handicap. The practice has had an important influence on social behaviour and on family life, as well as on economic and national development. Previous ethnographic and anthropological accounts of female mutilation (written mainly in the colonial period) have tended to treat it as a symbolic cultural ritual from ancient times, and to ignore its economic and social significance.

Since the custom itself and the culture from which it originates are largely unknown to Western writers and researchers, the basic information provided in many reports is both biased and exaggerated. Moreover, most of the literature available has used similar references and fails to distinguish between the historical distribution of the custom in the past and its contemporary prevalence. Knowledge of the operation involved derives mainly from the scanty literature written by male medical doctors, the majority of whom were Europeans who served in the colonial administration in those regions where the custom is practiced. Their reports and case studies are almost exclusively descriptions of the medical problems and clinical evidence of the operations.

Among the early writers on female circumcision (mainly Europeans), were Remondino, 1891; Sequeira, 1931; Melly, 1935; Worsley, 1938; Abu-Shamma, 1949; and Laycock, 1950. During the last 15 years, most critics of the practice are African and Arab physicians and social scientists who have shown a deep concern about the continuation of the custom. These agitators, both men and women, wrote critical reports about the practice and carried out valuable research which has contributed first-hand facts and information towards its study. Among these are: Drs. Karim and Ammar, who carried out comprehensive research on 'Female Circumcision and Sexual Desire', in Egypt in 1965; Dr. Shandall, who conducted impressive research on the adverse effects of 'Female Circumcision and Infibulation in the Sudan' in 1967; so far, only Dr. T. Baashir has studied the 'Psychological Aspects of Female Circumcision', among Egyptian and Sudanese women in 1976. There are several other Sudanese doctors who have written about the medical aspect of the practice, such as Dr. Mustafa in 1966, Dr. Modawi in 1973, Dr. Bakar 1979, and Dr. G. Badri.

Among the active women's groups in the countries concerned who speak and write against the custom are: Awa Thiam, a Senegalese sociologist who wrote *La Parole Aux Negresses*, in 1978, in which the major topics are polygamy and the genital mutilation of African women; Dr. Nawal of Egypt devoted a chapter on 'Circumcision of Girls', in her book *The Hidden Face of Eve: Women in the Arab World*, 1980; M.B. Assaad, an Egyptian social scientist, has undertaken a pilot study and written a paper on 'Female Circumcision in Egypt, Current Research and Social Implications', 1979; Dr. A. Asma El Dareer carried out research in the Sudan on 'The Prevalence and Epidemiology of Female Circumcision' in 1980. Also, a number of Arab and African women have written articles about the ill-effects of the practice. In addition, Esther Ogunmodrel, a Nigerian journalist wrote an article 'Women against Mutilation'; Edna Adan, an experienced Somali midwife and health worker, wrote about the health consequences of infibulation in Somalia.

Despite the scarcity and short-comings of available literature on female circumcision, many of these studies and reports give an accurate picture and provide important information about the practice, and it is through these that I have gained an understanding and overview of the practice, its effects on health, and the prevalence of the operations.

To the best of my knowledge, this study is the first of its kind on Somalia. For the first time, comprehensive information about female mutilation is presented in a coordinated form which takes account of the socio-cultural and historical features, instead of simply looking at the practice in isolation. The few studies or reports on this practice in Somalia [Melly, 1935; Laycock, 1950; Pieters, 1977; Otoo, 1977] and the M.D. dissertations of three Somali medical students in 1979 are all by male doctors who focussed only on its medical aspects and its ill effects. As men, and mostly foreigners, these doctors were not able to interview the women. They relied on male informants, secondary sources and on case histories of the women patients they saw in hospitals. Most of them had never even had the opportunity to see the operation performed on young girls; they only dealt with the complications arising from it.

Infibulation is the most sensitive aspect of Somali culture that a man, and especially a foreigner, can investigate. The practice has always been closely guarded from foreign scrutiny. Unlike the Sudan and other parts of Africa, the colonial administration, whether British, Italian or French, never attempted to interfere with this custom. These reasons make it difficult for foreigners, men or women, to investigate this subject as it is quite impossible for them to collect data on the issue.

Examples of such attempts include Dr. Pieters' article on 'Infibulation in the Horn of Africa', which appeared in the *New York State Journal of Medicine*, April 1977 (pp.729–32). It is not based on facts, even though Fran Hosken has, unfortunately, referred to it in the case histories in her report on 'Genital and Sexual Mutilation of Females'. The report is exaggerated and misinformed, and can only be regarded as Western propaganda. In the case of Somalia, some of the inaccurate information reported by Dr. Pieters and subsequently referred to by Fran Hosken is that: '*After each divorce*, the woman is immediately reinfibulated to restore her to the *original condition of virginity*, at least in appearance, and thus enabling her *father to collect another bride-price*.' (Emphasis in original.) But in Somalia, infibulation takes place only once: before marriage; bride-price is, as a rule, only paid for the first marriage when the girl is a virgin. If other marriages occur, generally the father has less power over his daughter and the woman has more choice in determining her future, there is no more bargaining about bride-price.

Another false statement from these reports states that: 'Dr. Pieters briefly discussed the psychology effects of these horrible mutilations and he states that the *unusual sadness* of Somali women, *who always seem depressed*, is frequently described *in literary works*. Young Somali women who are among the most beautiful in Africa, "*never smile*", and they are of an "*astonishing coldness*" ' he states. (Author's emphasis.)

These are not only inaccuracies but also present an unscientific analysis and result in a distorted view of the lives of the women of a whole nation. This type of misinformation and misinterpretation can carry implications of racism and cultural imperialism that can only be counter-productive to our aims of change. It can create a general misunderstanding, and is of no value as a contribution to Somalia's attempt to foment change.

However, the time has now come for Somali women themselves to carry out studies and research which will lead to their own liberation, and that of the future generations of women.

This study is not an end, but a beginning. It will be up-dated and revised continuously as more facts and information come to light and as women begin to speak out for themselves.

1. Circumcision and Infibulation of Women in Somalia

Throughout human history, mankind has developed many customs and traditions, which are related to social organization and cultural codes of behaviour. Of these ancient customs, while many have disappeared or were gradually abandoned, others remained. Female circumcision is one custom that still survives.

Definition and Types of Female Circumcision

Dr. Gerard Zwang, in his article on 'Female Sexual Mutilations, Technique and Results', wrote: '*Any definitive and irremediable removal of a healthy organ is a mutilation.*' (Emphasis in original.) [Zwang: 1977: 1]. The normal female external genital organ is constituted by the vulva, which comprises the labia majora, the labia minora or nymphs, and the clitoris, covered by its prepuce, in front of the vestibule of the urinary meatus and the vaginal orifice. (See Figure 1a.) In women the constitution of the vulva is genetically programmed and is identically reproduced in all the embryos and in all races. The vulva is an integral part of the natural physical possessions of women; when *normal* there is absolutely no reason, *medical*, *moral* or *aesthetic*, to *suppress* all or any part of these exterior genital organs. Therefore, 'this intervention is *mutilation*.' [Zwang: 1971] (See Figure 1a.)

According to Webster's Dictionary, to mutilate (from 'mutilius' — maimed) means to deprive, to cut off or permanently destroy a limb or an essential part, to cripple, to cut or alter radically so as to make imperfect by removing part or parts, to cause permanent damage.

Dr. Verzin in his article on 'Sequelae of Female Circumcision', summarized the medical facts of genital mutilation of girls and women and the resulting complications arising from the practice. He stated that the term 'female circumcision' includes all operations involving mutilation of the female genitalia [1975:163]. Most medical authorities distinguish two main mutilations, excision and infibulation. Excision, or clitoridectomy, is the partial or complete removal of the clitoris only, to the full excision of the clitoris and the labia minora. Infibulation or occlusion, means excision plus stitching and reducing the size of the orifice of the vulva.

From this description we can see that female circumcision is the popular term, loosely applied to a variety of mutilating operations performed on women by many different ethnic populations. Three main types of female circumcision operations are described in the medical literature and classified according to the consequent severity of mutilation. The classifications of Dr. Shandall (1967), followed by Dr. Verzin (1975), and Dr. Cook (1976), are adopted here:

Type 1 – Circumcision

This mildest form of female circumcision consists of removal of the prepuce of the clitoris only, preserving the clitoris itself and the posterior larger parts of the labia minora. This type of operation is also known as *Sunna*, which means 'Tradition' in Arabic.

Many medical authorities believe the aim of this operation corresponds to that of the circumcision of the male prepuce or foreskin of the penis. To me and to many others, the aim and results of any form of circumcision of women are quite different from those applying to the circumcision of men.

Type 2 – Excision or Clitoridectomy

This type is more severe, entailing the ablation of the clitoris. It consists of the partial or total removal of the clitoris together with the adjacent tissues of the labia minora (small lips) and sometimes the whole of it, except the labia majora (large lips) and without closure of the vulva.

Dr. Baashir, in his article 'Psychological Aspects of Female Circumcision' noted that the term 'female circumcision' has varying connotations which may be a significant reflection of practices. He explained that in classical Arabic, female excision or clitoridectomy is called *khefad* which literally means 'reduction'. In physical terms, he continued, it thus indicates partial reduction of the clitoris. This

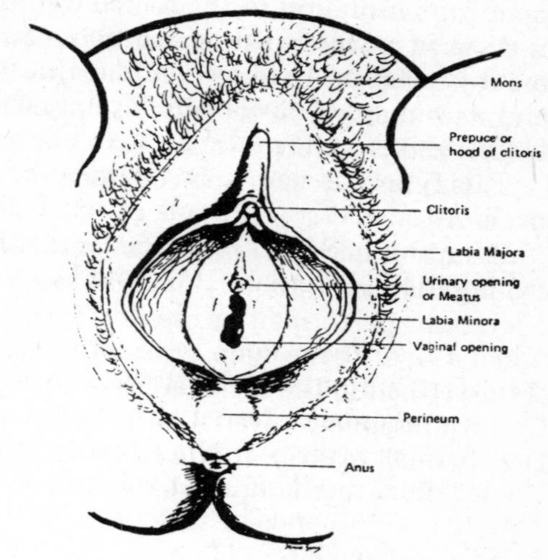

Normal Adolescent Vulva
in extension

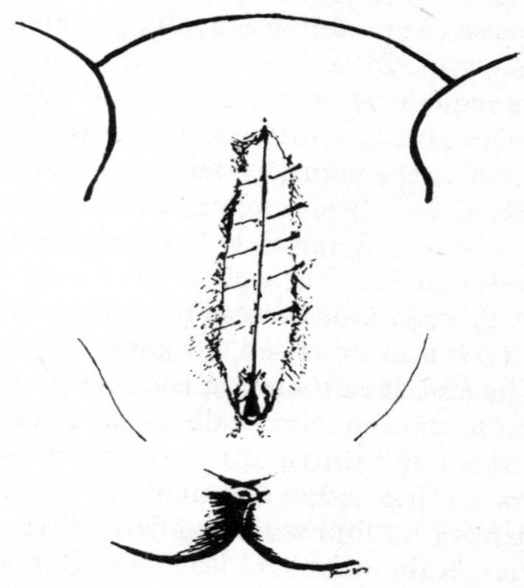

Infibulated Vulva

particular practice is usually based on an unconfirmed interpretation of the Prophet Mohamed saying to Om Attiya, a female practitioner of circumcision, 'reduce but do not destroy'. There is no valid evidence that the Prophet made any specific pronouncement in relation to female circumcision, but partial clitoridectomy and its variations have been popular, and practised in some Islamic countries, and known as 'Sunna'. [Baashir, 1977:3].

This type was said to be the most common in Egypt before its prohibition and still prevails to some extent. It is also replacing infibulation in Sudan since the legislation of 1946 which prohibits infibulation [Shandall, 1967 and El Dareer, 1979].

Type 3 – Infibulation

The term 'infibulation' is derived from the name given to the Roman practice of fastening a 'fibula' or 'clasp' through the large lips of their wives genitalia in order to prevent them from having illicit sexual intercourse. It was also said that a ring was pushed through the prepuce of men, usually slaves. [Sequeira, 1931: 1054; Hosken, 1979: 2].

Infibulation is also called Pharaonic circumcision. From all the medical descriptions this is the most severe and drastic form of genital mutilation. It involves excision plus infibulation. It is the common form used in Somalia and Sudan. The two operations, excision and infibulation, may be associated in some ways. Thus some medical authorities have indicated that among the Kikuyu, the occurrence of infibulation is usually as a consequence of careless, over extensive excision, while among the Somalis excision is intended to facilitate occlusion. (Laycock, 1950:444). In Somalia infibulation is known as *Gudniin* meaning the Somali infibulation.

In the Sudan they called it Pharaonic circumcision,[1] but in Egypt today, it is referred to as 'Sudanese' circumcision because it is no longer practised in Egypt.

The aim of infibulation is to encase the clitoris, the labia minora, and the inner walls of the labia majora (at least the anterior two thirds). The two sides of the vulva are finally attached to each other, either by stitching with silk or catgut sutures[2] (in the Sudan) or by thorns (in Somalia), thus reducing the size of the orifice of the vulva and leaving only a very small opening at the lower end to allow for the passage of urine and menstrual flow (see Figure 1b).

In the other two types of circumcision no particular aftercare is essential other than to prevent excessive bleeding. Usually, traditional herbs and local medicines believed to enhance healing are applied to the wound. For the Pharaonic operation, as already indicated, the surgery is more severe and therefore, more immediate treatment and aftercare are necessary.

Age At Which Female Circumcision Is Performed

The age at which these operations are done varies from area to area according to the type of procedure and local traditions. Such an operation may be performed as early as the eighth day after birth, or at puberty, or after the girl herself gives birth to a child, or in some cases, soon after marriage.

In most areas however, the operation is performed in childhood — between the age of three and eight — as Dr. Verzin has briefly summarized:

8th day after birth	—	Ethiopia
10 weeks after birth	—	Arabia
3–4 years (Type I and II)	—	Somalia
3–8 years	—	Egypt
5–8 years	—	Sudan
8–10 years (Type III)	—	Somalia
Shortly after marriage	—	Masai tribes
After bearing first child	—	Some tribes in Guinea[3]

Most female circumcision operations are performed by traditional practitioners without anaesthetic (except in recent years in some well-to-do families). Among such societies, a girl will be considered unclean, improper or unmarriageable if she does not undergo this operation.

Extent of the Practice in Africa and Elsewhere

A global review of female mutilation today shows that the custom is mainly practised in the continent of Africa. It is also common in the southern part of the Arab peninsula and along the Persian Gulf, in the Middle East, and among the Muslim population of Indonesia and Malaysia.

Africa

In Africa the record shows that female mutilation is practised in a wide area from the Horn of Africa and the Red Sea stretching to the Equator. From Egypt and Sudan in the north, to Kenya and Tanzania in East Africa, to the West African coast; from Sierra

Leone to Mauritania and in all countries in between, including Nigeria, Mozambique in the south, Botswana and Lesotho.

The map shows the areas affected according to the forms of mutilation practised (see Figure 2). There are, however, exceptions; in many African countries not all the women are subjected to this practice, but only those of certain tribes. For instance, it is reported that among the Ino, in Kenya, the second largest ethnic group after the Kikuyu, neither men nor women are circumcised [Hosken, 1979:18].

The most common type of female genital mutilation practised in Africa today is Type II, clitoridectomy or excision, which is reported to be used in more than 20 countries (see Figure 2).[4]

The Sunna variant is also popular in South Yemen (Aden), Oman, Egypt and Sudan. In its mildest form the Sunna type is also reported to be practised by the Muslims in Indonesia and Malaysia.

Infibulation is commonly practised in Somalia and wherever ethnic Somalis live (Jibouti, Ethiopia, Kenya). It is also practised among the northern Muslim Sudanese and in some parts of Upper Egypt. In West Africa infibulation is at present reported among some Muslim groups in Mali and in Nigeria. [Shandall, 1967:180; Hosken, 1979:6].

In Somalia, practically every girl without exception is circumcised and the majority are infibulated. In Jibouti and all other parts where there are Somali ethnic groups excision and infibulation are universal, and similar to those in the Somali Democratic Republic. The operation is performed on young girls before the age of puberty and usually with no ritual.

In the Sudan, in spite of the law of 1945 prohibiting Pharaonic circumcision, infibulation still continues, although the wide prevalence of infibulation is reported to be replaced by Type II or clitoridectomy. [Shandall, 1967:184; El Dareer, 1977:2].

In Egypt, despite many years of education,[5] awareness and modernization of Egyptian society, genital mutilation is still reported from the Nile Valley. As told by Hansen [1972:4] until the 1920s, almost every girl in Egypt was circumcised. There is also enough scattered data to support the opinion that there are more circumcised than uncircumcised women in Egypt. The most reliable sources are gynaecologists, Mother and Child Health Centres and family planning centres, as well as the studies and reports undertaken by Sadawi, Assaad and Baashir, who confirmed that the Sunna type circumcision is still performed on

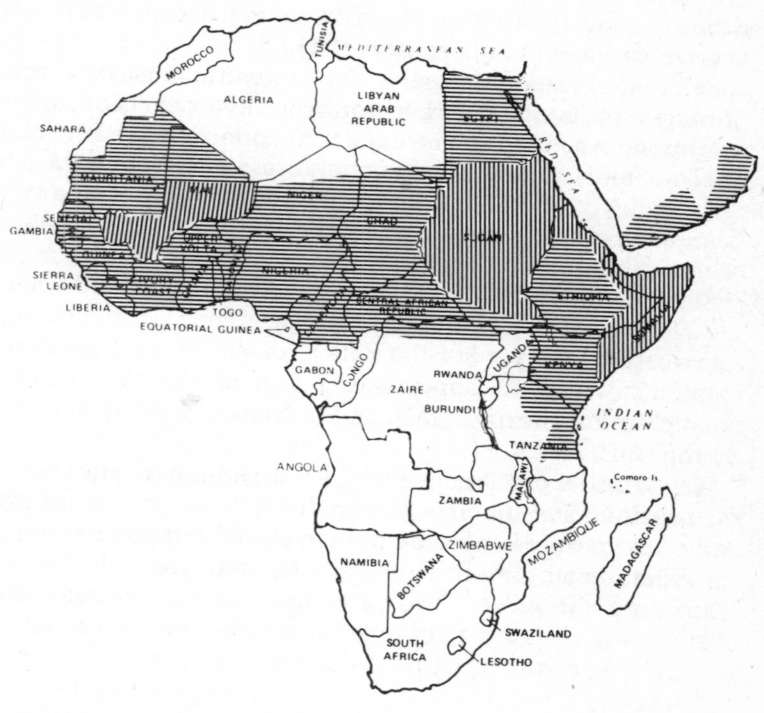

areas where most women are infibulated

excision and circumcision widespread

some cases reported

at least 75% of the women and girls of Egypt. Only the upper class and privileged few are spared.

Infibulation is also reported from the Upper Nile Valley — Nubia [Kennedy, 1970] and in 1979 Family Planning Clinics that are beginning to reach rural areas, confirmed this.

Ethiopia: Dr. Melly (1935) and Dr. Huber (1964) who worked in Ethiopia reported that infibulation is practised among the Muslim population such as the Somalis, Danakil, Harari and Galla. Huber added that excision is practised by other ethnic groups regardless of religion; it is called *Girz* in Amharic. According to Huber, among the Amharas, in the highlands, girls are usually excised at about 8–15 days old and in some areas at about 40 days old.

Eritrea: Excision is more commonly practised, but also on occasion infibulation is performed, mostly by the Muslim groups. [Shandall, 1967:180].

Kenya: Different forms of female circumcision are practised by many tribes here. The operation is of great importance to the upland Bantu, the highlands, and many of the plain Nilotes and by the Gusii and Kuria of South Nyanza. [Murray, 1974].

The Bantu word *Irua* can be translated both as 'initiation' and as 'excision'. The practice among the Kikuyu was described by Jomo Kenyatta. He stressed the significance of the custom among the Kikuyu and stated: 'No proper Kikuyu would dream of marrying a girl who has not been circumcised, and vice versa. It is taboo for a Kikuyu man or woman to have sexual relations with someone who has not undergone this operation.' [Kenyatta, 1938:132].

Although the British administration and Missionary Society's campaign against female circumcision in the 1920s and 1930s had some impact in the urban areas, female circumcision operations still prevail in the rural areas today.

Nigeria: Genital mutilation is reported to be practised by many ethnic groups, such as the Yoruba, who were reported to excise girls, usually on the sixth day after birth. [Longo, 1964:470–75]. Some sources also reported that the Hausa, and the Ibos also excise their girls. Infibulation is said to be generally practised in the Muslim north. [Hosken, 1978].

Sierra Leone: Most ethnic groups practice certain forms of genital mutilation. [Hosken, 1978]. Their girls are initiated at puberty in a secret ceremony in which only initiated women of the same ethnic group may participate. Female mutilation continues today in all areas of the country. This is confirmed by a report provided by *Kankalay*, the Sierra Leone Muslim Men and Women's Association.

Mali: Female circumcision is practised in Mali today among many ethnic groups, such as the Bambora, Seracola, Malinke, Songhoinsdi and Peul. [Imperalo, 1977; Hosken, 1979]. Both the practice of excision and infibulation are strongly established in Mali society. Though some traditional practices have recently been relaxed, practically all women in Mali are excised, except those who belong to the Sonrai ethnic group.

Senegal: In most rural areas in Senegal female excision is practised, with the exception of those in the Dakar area. According to Madame N'Deaije, Deputy Chief, School of Midwives, about a quarter of the women who come to the maternity hospital in Dakar are excised.

The Wolof and Serere peoples, who are the majority and live mainly in the Dakar area, do not practice any form of mutilation. Other ethnic groups, such as the Toucouleur who live along the Senegal river, practice infibulation, while in West Senegal the Mandingo and Casamas excise their girls. The Fulani (17.5%) of the Senegalese population also practice excision on their girls and women.

Ivory Coast: Female circumcision is widely practised in the Ivory Coast (according to a recent survey on 'Genital Mutilation' [Hosken, 1979], especially among the northern tribes such as Guen. The type of the operation depends on the tribe, and permission for the operation is usually given by the village chiefs.

Excision is mostly common among the Muslim groups, such as the Malinke, all of whose girls must undergo excision. This is reported to take place as a village puberty rite with celebrations, but also the operation is sometimes performed on younger girls at the age of six years. [Hosken, 1977].

Upper Volta: According to an article on female excision in Upper Volta in *Famille et Developpement* [Taoko, 1977:16] the women of all ethnic groups are excised and it is especially important to the Mossi, the largest and dominant group in the country; they believe that the clitoris is a dangerous organ which can cause impotence in men and kills babies at birth. The excision operation in Upper Volta usually takes place outside the village under a tree; razors, knives and traditional herbs are used in its performance.

The foregoing cites only some examples of the extent of female mutilation in Africa,[6] but there are other countries in the continent (see map, Fig.2) where the practice is recorded.

The Arab Peninsula

Type 1 genital mutilations are recorded throughout the southern part of the Arab Peninsula, Aden and Hadramout, according to the report on the Arab Peninsula submitted to the WHO Seminar in Khartoum in February 1979.

Another cruel custom that is practised in Southern Yemen and along the Persian Gulf is to put salt into the vagina after childbirth. The reason behind this is that it induces narrowing of the vagina (stenosis). According to women's beliefs the main purpose of this is to restore the vagina to its former shape and size and make intercourse more pleasurable for the husband.

Musqat-Oman: In Oman, which borders Southern Yemen and extends to the entrance of the Persian Gulf, Type I female circumcision, as well as putting salt into the vagina after childbirth, is also practised.

Asia

According to available medical information, female genital operations are, at present, confirmed in only two countries in South East Asia, namely Indonesia and Malaysia. It is also reported that this custom is practised only by the Muslim population in these countries.

According to physicians, the type of circumcision performed in these areas is not as drastic and harmful as those in Africa. They state that it usually takes place immediately, or shortly after the child is born, and is performed by either a woman village healer (*dukun wanita*) or a midwife. They use a very simple technique, namely cutting the top of the gland very slightly, sometimes the clitoris itself is cut, along with the labia minora. It is said that in some cases, no cutting takes place, but that only a drop of blood is produced by sticking a needle into the gland.[7]

In Indonesia and Malaysia, female circumcision is not an indigenous practice but was imported with Islam. In Africa it was practised before the advent of Islam.

The Western World

The idea of controlling women's sexuality seems to be common to most men in all societies. The methods used in the West are different from those used in Oriental and African countries, but the aims are generally the same.

In this context, clitoridectomy is not entirely strange to Western countries, though many Western readers seem to be horrified to hear of such customs and practices. In England and America it was said that a large number of such operations were performed especially in the second half of the 19th Century. One school of thought held that clitoridectomy was necessary to cure such sexual aberrations as 'nymphomania', and also to prevent all kinds of other physical diseases and emotional disorders (*hysteria, masturbation* and other non-conforming behaviour). [Kati David]. Possibly there are women living in America and Europe today who have suffered this form (as well as other more familiar forms) of gynophobic, medically unnecessary mutilating surgery. The repression of women's sexuality by various means and methods occurs almost everywhere, and exists in all patriarchal societies throughout history and up to the present day.

Type and Frequency of Circumcision of Women in Somalia

Female circumcision is almost universal among the Somalis. [Melly, 1935; Laycock, 1950; S. Otoo, 1977; my own findings, 1980]. Infibulation or Pharaonic circumcision is the type generally practised by all the ethnic groups of Somalia; no girl can expect to grow to the age of puberty without undergoing this operation.

Boys as well as girls in Somalia undergo circumcision as a vital element of socialization in the Somali culture. Usually no ceremony accompanies these operations, except in some parts of the south, where a feast and celebration takes place after the operations. Sheep or goats are killed for a feast for the relatives and friends of the children. The abundance of the feast and the number of animals slaughtered depends on the wealth of the families. Children may be circumcised in a group or individually. Among the nomads in the north, the operation can also be performed upon a group of girls from the same extended family or upon just an individual, but in either case it takes place in isolated places. The operation is initiated and performed without fuss or feasts, although the occasion has a special significance and there is some preparation. It is usually performed in the cool, early morning. The above description applies both to boys and girls.

Circumcision of girls takes place when they are between the ages of 6 and 12. The only reason suggested for the choice of this particular age is that up to the twelfth year a girl may be regarded as small and undeveloped and thus safe from male attention. Also, it seems that as a result of generations of experience, it has been found that young girls of such an age are able to withstand the shock and after-effects of the operation.

Operations as Performed by the Traditional Midwife

The little girl is made to sit on a very low stool; then the woman 'operator' sits in front of the child with her special razor blade, or knife in some cases. The child's legs are drawn apart and each one is held by one or two strong women relatives or friends. Two or more women hold the little girl's arms and shoulders and one holds her head pinning her back to the ground. The girl is held tightly in order to stop her from struggling and also to expose her vulva for the operation. The operator then is able to manipulate the vulva with her razor blade and first excises the clitoris. At that stage, the operator as well as the other women around the girl shout out an ululating chorus of chants of victory and encouragement, because this is thought to be the act of purification and it also helps to quieten and drown the cries and screams of the child. The operator then starts to excise the labia minora and various parts of the labia majora.[8] All this is done without any anaesthetic or antiseptic precautions. The women continue ululating and giving advice and encouragement to the girl until the operation is complete.

To sew up or fasten together the raw edges of the labia majora, the traditional midwife uses vegetable thorns which she prepares beforehand and brings with her. She inserts them on opposite sides, usually about 4–6 of them on each side, leaving an outlet for urine and the later menstrual flow so small as to admit no more than a fingertip.

After the thorns are inserted, the midwife winds a string or thread around the thorns to hold them in position (the same way that shoes are laced). The raw area is then covered with cloth soaked in special oil and local herbs such as 'malmal' (a paste mixture made from sugar and gum). This dressing adheres to the wound and adequately controls haemorrhage.

When the operation has been completed the girl's legs are tied together from the waist to the toes; she is then carried into an isolated place already prepared for her. She lies on her back on a mat with several pillows to support her sides and back and remains like that for several (3-4) days. The patient is given a special diet during the first 3-4 days after the operation, designed to avoid frequent bowel movements. She is given hot porridge with pure animal 'ghee' (Somali butter) soon after the operation on the first day and she takes little fluid, only a few sips of water at a time. When urinating she lies on one side while her thighs are still tied together.

Three to four days after the operation, the thorns and other dressings on the wound are moistened with oil and then carefully removed. The binder is put back on her thighs, but loosely this time so that she can move slowly, supported by a stick. At this stage, she is also allowed to sleep on her side.

No male is normally allowed to be in the vicinity during the operation, nor to see the girl until she has recovered and returns to normal activities. No unmarried girl is permitted to watch the scene, especially those who have not been circumcised. On the 10th to 14th day after the operation, all binders are removed and then she can begin to take short steps or walk about without the aid of a stick.[9]

After-care in the Infibulation Operation

It is most important that the child patient passes urine within six hours after the operation; this is to ensure whether or not the passage left for the flow of urine is blocked. The patient is taken off her bedding and made to rest on one thigh or buttock with the lower limbs still tied and is then encouraged to urinate or otherwise risk being taunted and ridiculed as cowardly. Water may be poured nearby to stimulate micturition. Urination is really very painful and many young girls refuse to pass water for 2-3 days; serious suffering can result and some are even taken to hospital in urban sectors. In these cases secondary infection is reported to be the rule.

Disinfectants are, of course, unknown in the rural homes, but during the first few days, traditional aromatic herbs (e.g. asal) and dried sap (e.g. fah) are burned below the child, with the intention that the rising fumes will help the healing process, and dissipate bad odours resulting from coagulation of blood and stale urine.

In the rural areas to show that a little girl is not yet circumcised her hair is usually shaved in a distinctive way: i.e. an inner ring, extending over the vertex of the skull, is shaved while the outer part of the hair is cut short with long tufts left on the crown of the head. After the operation, and as a sign that she is infibulated, her head is completely shaved and the hair is then allowed to grow long so that it may be arranged into a beautiful traditional style and left to hang over the girl's shoulders.

If the infibulation operation is not successful, as judged by the healing process, it is repeated. In my interviews, I came across women and girls who were operated on not once but two, and even three times. The main purpose of the operation is to achieve a small opening, just big enough to permit urine and menstrual blood to flow out. Family honour depends on making the opening as small as possible, because for the Somalis, the smaller this artificial passage the greater is the girl's value and reputation. These infibulation operations described above continue to be performed today throughout the country

The Operators of Female Circumcision

These operations have usually been performed by middle-aged, illiterate women who have acquired their skill through apprenticeship to become experienced practitioners. The traditional midwives usually earn their living by such operations (infibulation and defibulation at the time of marriage), child deliveries, massaging and other similar activities.

In some parts of the country, these types of traditional surgeons came from a particular ethnic group; whereas in other parts it could be anyone, often specialized in circumcision and other traditional surgery, who earned his/her livelihood by that means. Their fee for the job in the urban areas is money and gifts, and in the rural areas, food or livestock.

More recently, in the urban areas, elderly, trained midwives have gradually replaced traditional practitioners. They have learned the method by themselves, mostly by observation. There is also evidence that nowadays, even male nurses are in competition with midwives, and circumcise both boys and girls. These new, trained medical personnel, of course, operate privately in more hygienic conditions. They use local anaesthetics to enable them to avoid unnecessary pain and they also give anti-tetanus injections, and a course of antibiotics is administered after the operation. The danger that arises from the use of the anaesthetics is that the patient cannot struggle or protest: surgeons may, therefore, remove too much tissue, so that many mothers do not like, or have fears about the new method. These modern practices apply mainly in the urban areas, but the traditional, painful method still continues to be practised in the countryside and remote areas.

Defibulation

Infibulation (sewing up) is usually reversed by 'defibulation' (consisting of making a short incision to separate the fused labia minora) at the time of marriage. This is done by a traditional midwife or in recent years by a trained midwife, or by the husband. This separation of the vulva is incomplete, so that at childbirth a further incision is often necessary to allow the baby to emerge. After the birth of every child, the woman has to be stitched close again.

Effects on Health, the Psychological Condition of Children, Married Life, and Child Bearing

A complete list of complications has been reported in the medical literature. The commonest are seen in hospitals and health centres by gynaecologists, and are derived from observations and case histories.

Those I shall describe here will be based on the most important medical publications on genital operations from 1950 to 1977, which provide a comprehensive summary of the facts of the health conditions of women subjected to genital mutilations, especially the most drastic type; 'Pharaonic' circumcision.

The complications are numerous and can be classified into three categories, namely: immediate; delayed or remote; psychological results.

Immediate Complications

Shock: The extent of shock after the operation is out of proportion to the amount of haemorrhage. The shock is mainly due to fear, pain and, most likely, loss of blood (in the majority of cases no anaesthetic is used).

Haemorrhage: Uncontrollable bleeding may occur from injury to

the dorsal artery of the clitoris or from the labial branches of the pudendal artery. More commonly it comes from the leach of veins in the labia and clitoris.
Injuries: Damage to the urethral meatus, Bartholin gland and the duct, the perineum or sometimes the rectum, are liable to occur as a result of the little girl's struggles.
Infection: Infection is reported by many medical authorities; this occurred in between 7% and 10% of Shandall's case histories, including fatal cases of tetanus, due to unsterilized tools in many cases. Furthermore, the tight bandaging of the legs to keep the edges of the flesh together is likely to interfere with the drainage of the wound. Infection may lead to total failure of the wound edges to heal, or to healing in patches giving the midline scar a perforated appearance. Instead of one stream of urine, there is a simultaneous trickle through several exits. Infection may travel beyond the vulva. Because of the bad downward drainage, due to the restriction of the bandaging and the enforced position of the patient after the operation, extension of infection upward to the cervix, uterus and tubes, may occur. This spread of infection from the vulva to the immature vaginal epithelium may cause a severe type of vaginitis.
Retention of Urine: This is reported as a fairly common complication arising during the first 48 hours after circumcision. Such cases are commonly seen in hospitals for treatment. Retention of urine may be due to a combination of fear, pain of passing urine through the sore area, or sometimes due to occlusion of the fistula by local sepsis which causes oedema, inflammatory exudate, granulation tissue or fibrosis. The retained urine can easily become infected and the infection may spread upward. [Verzin, 1975; Shandall, 1967; Modawi, 1973].

Delayed or Remote Complications: Malformation of External Genitalia

Strictly speaking, this is not a complication since it is, of course, universal to all circumcised women, being maximal in Pharaonic and least in the Sunna type of operations. In the uncomplicated case, the final result is a flattened vulva without labia majora and minora, and made up of a membrane of skin marked by a midline scar extending backwards from the symphysis pubis to about half an inch from the perineum.

The urinary meatus is hidden by this skin diaphragm and the vulva orifice is tightly scarred and of a size that admits

> only the index finger. But for the reduced orifice, the overall appearance is somewhat reminiscent of that seen after a badly performed vulvectomy. The newcomer to gynaecological practice among races who subject their womenfolk to this ritual cannot but be impressed by the appearance of the end result of circumcision. Bimanual examination has to be made with the index finger only. In many cases even this is not possible, and rectal examination is used as a substitute. Similarly, per speculum examination and exposure of the cervix in the clinic have often to be abandoned. [Verzin, 1975:163].

The statements above could undoubtedly be further elaborated but enough has been said to indicate the serious physical handicap and distortion caused to the women's natural functions, despite differences in the extent of the mutilation. For many years now, despite the alarm that has been expressed at the widespread physical damage due to female circumcision, people have continued to cling to their old custom involving women's sexual mutilation. Furthermore, in addition to the malformation of external genitalia, the following remote complications can result from this practice.

Keloid Scarring: This is a common phenomenon of circumcision, especially among women of Negroid blood. Laycock and Shandall believe that it is due to incomplete healing, especially after infection. The scars are not important in themselves, but they make surgery more difficult. [Verzin, 1975; Modawi, 1974]. It was reported that Keloid[10] formation is about ten times more common in scars of Pharaonic circumcision than in Sunna circumcision.

Vulval Cysts and Vulval Abscesses: Implantation dermoid cysts formation are the commonest complications of circumcision, particularly of the Pharaonic type. The cause is seen to arise from the edges of the incision, which is sometimes turned inwards while being sutured. The cysts may vary in size up to that of a football and when large, they hang down and cover the introitus. They occasionally become infected and present abscesses which require incision. [Verzin; Laycock]. Modawi reported eight cases of dermoid cysts in his series, six with abscesses. Shandall reported 53 among 3,800 patients, of whom 51 out of 3,013 cases were infibulated and only two out of the remaining 807 cases had Type I and Type II circumcision.

Chronic Pelvic Infections: According to Shandall, chronic pelvic infection is three times more common among infibulated women than in all other groups. In some cases it is reported to be the result of an acute ascending genital tract infection at the time of circumcision [Verzin]. Shandall believes that infibulation brings about this high incidence of pelvic infection in three ways: infection at the time of circumcision; interference with drainage of urine and vaginal secretions by the vulval skin diaphragm; and infection of the split and resutured circumcision wound after labour.

Coital Difficulties: These are common, though rarely mentioned by the patient. Where infibulation is practiced, the first penetration of the introitus is supposed to occur during the consummation of marriage. In the southern region of Somalia and in the Sudan, the husband expects the concomitant difficulty of penetration, and if he fails to accomplish coitus with his new bride, it is regarded as a disgrace to his virility. In this regard the husband may force the barrier, and cause a laceration which may involve perineum, and sometimes, more seriously, damage the rectum and even urethra. Dysparoeunia and vaginisimus may follow. Sometimes the scar fails to dilate in the centre and then repeated pressure in the site causes stretching and invagination of the skin and a false vaginal canal is formed. The couple are usually unaware of the condition. Sometimes, after repeated attempts at penetration, the husband approaches his bride through the anus and gets some satisfaction.

Funnel anus, anal fissures and occasionally incompetent anal sphincter, all due to anal intercourse, are reported to occur in cases of tight circumcision where vaginal intercourse is impossible. [Shandall, 1967; Modawi, 1973; Verzin, 1975]. Unhappy marriages are sometimes due to tight circumcision. Failure of penetration and the lack of sexual satisfaction of the husband may be taken as a cause of frequent divorces.

The husband, in a blind attempt to open the introitus, may use a sharp instrument and injure the adjacent parts. Very rarely the couple may secretly approach a midwife, to do the defibulation (in the case of Sudan, Ethiopia and southern regions of Somalia). In northern regions of Somalia and in Jibouti, usually the bride must be re-opened by cutting the opening to allow intra-vaginal penetration. This operation is most commonly performed by the traditional midwife. In recent times in the urban areas the couple go to the hospital or call a trained midwife to perform the operation at home. Injury, infection and cases of severe haemorrhag have been known under both circumstances especially when performed by a traditional midwife.

Lack of Orgasm: The few studies that have been made on female circumcision reported the absence of orgasm to be extremely common, probably because of the lack of a clitoris.

Research[11] of 651 circumcised women, to study sexual behaviour in excised women, showed that circumcision has a definite effect on female orgasm. The study showed that only 41.1% of the group reached orgasm; whilst according to the *Kinsey Report* the figure is 70–77% for non-circumcised women. The research on circumcised women also showed that different degrees of mutilation were reflected in levels of sexual response, and indicated that the presence of part of the clitoris and labia minora gave increased frequency of orgasm.

Another research project[12] involving 4,024 women in Sudan showed that the majority (80%) of those who were Pharaonically circumcised reported that they never experienced orgasm and claimed to have no idea of what an orgasm was. Among the Sunna circumcised sample (807) about 12% reported not reaching orgasm at all and only 7% of the total sample of the uncircumcised group (204) had never experienced orgasm.

In addition to these results, the reports of Masters and Johnson, the *Kinsey Report* and the *Hite Report* all proved that no matter in which parts of their body women experienced orgasm, it was directly or indirectly as a result of clitoral stimulation. This means that the clitoris, the labia minora, the labia majora and the Bartholins glands are the primary areas of sexual stimulation. In other words, clitoral stimulation evokes orgasm in women though it may be experienced deeper in the body, around the vagina and other structures.

Both men and women have been conditioned and misled into believing that orgasm is due to friction against the walls of the vagina and only results from the use of the penis during intercourse. Due to this, men's interpretation of sexuality, the vaginal orgasm, has become a centre of controversy. The fact is, that there cannot be a vaginal orgasm because the vagina has no nerve ends. It is the clitoris that has the nerve endings or the sensual capacity to be the main focus or creator of orgasm.

Like the penis, it is a network of nerves and blood vessels, and when these are charged with blood it swells and becomes hard and stiff. This phenomenon is called '*erection*' both in the clitoris and the penis and is the result of sexual stimulation, physical or psychic. Regardless of how friction is applied to the clitoris, i.e. by masturbation or by coitus, women's orgasm is almost always evoked by clitoral stimulation.

Thus, from the above, we can appreciate the importance of the clitoris to the attainment of a woman's full sexual satisfaction. It is now believed by many medical authorities that the majority of mutilated women are frigid, especially those with 'total clitoridectomy' and with other complex mutilations such as 'Pharaonic circumcision'.

As Dr. Gerard put it, 'A final anaesthesia of the clitoris takes place. The glans clitoridis has been amputated with its specific sensitive apparatus. No orgasm can be released by manipulation of what is no longer a primary erogenic zone, but an area of scarred tissue.' He continued to explain that the damage is the greater, as the woman has been mutilated at an early age before experimenting with adolescent clitoral masturbation or any other proper sexual function. [Gerard, 1977:0.12].

In many cases, infibulated women are reported to feel pain during the sexual act and, therefore, are unable to experience the slightest pleasure from penile penetration, or from solitary pelvic perineal rubbing.

In such a society, stated Dr. Verzin, 'the woman is regarded as a vessel for man's pleasure and subsequently the bearer of his offspring.' [Verzin, 1975:167].

Infertility: Both Verzin and Shandall reported that through tight introitus, dyspareunia and chronic pelvic infection, Pharaonic circumcision contributes to infertility.

Urinary Tract Infection: Because of the bridge of skin which hides the urinary meatus after the infibulation operation, the back flow of urine into the vagina and urethra results in a distorted stream, and there is a constant threat of bacterial infection. [Modawi, 1974; Verzin, 1975]. Shandall reports that 28% of patients with Pharaonic circumcision had bacteriologically positive urine cultures, compared to 8% of uncircumcised or Sunna circumcised women.

Obstetric Complications: Tight circumcision makes labour and proper vaginal examination extremely difficult. Sometimes it is reported that pregnancy might even take place in the absence of penetration, and cases were seen in labour with a pinhole introitus. [Verzin, 1975; Shandall, 1967; Modawi, 1974]. Due to the failure of the hardened scars to dilate, prolonged second-stage labour is common. Retention of urine during labour is also fairly common and catheterization is difficult. [Modawi, 1974; Verzin, 1975].

During labour two incisions of the circumcision scar are necessary an upward as well as a lateral or bilateral episiotomy to widen the vagina. If the anterior episiotomy is not done at the appropriate time, the head may be pushed through the perineum and leads to severe perineal lacerations. [Shandall, 1967; Modawi, 1974; Verzin, 1975].

According to many medical authorities, the following are the consequences of the anterior episiotomies:

Unnecessary blood loss [Shandall, 1967].
Bladder and urethral fistulae [Verzin, 1975].
Injury to the rectum [Laycock, 1950].
Late uterine prolapse [Laycock, 1950].
Local sepsis [Laycock, 1950; Modawi, 1974].

As anterior episiotomy is necessary for every childbirth, infection is common. Rectovaginal and vesico vaginal fistulae are reported [Verzin, 1975] resulting from obstructed labour (which sometimes leads to brain damage or loss of the baby).

Psychological Complications

This is an area in which no conclusive research has yet been made, nevertheless, it is hardly surprising that certain psychological reactions, ranging from temporary trauma and permanent frigidity to psychoses, occur among women who are subjected to this cruel operation. Despite what is known of the physical results of female mutilation, the psychological effects at an early age on the personality development of the young girl have been totally neglected. So far there is only one comprehensive study existing, by Dr. T.A. Baashir.

Dr. Baashir states that it is difficult to differentiate between the psychological effects and physical complications, since they are inseparable factors. Hence, he explained:

> Immediate complications of physical conditions such as haemorrhage, shock, septicaemia, retention of urine and tetanus may be seen as organic psychotic reactions, mainly in the form of toxic confusional states. On the other hand, psychiatric sequelae to incapacitating physical complications, such as haematacolpos, dermoid cysts, vesical fistulae, etc., may lead to chronic irritability, anxiety reactions, depressive episodes and even frank psychosis. [Baashir, 1977:4,5].

From this we can understand that the consequences for mental health arising out of circumcision include numerous injuries resulting from the agony confronted by the circumcised woman in every stage of her life: the effects of the circumcision and infibulation she has undergone in her youth; the constant worries of the painful monthly menstruation; the various sufferings she faces during marriage due to infibulation, such as the painful defibulation; the forceful penetration and sometimes physical assault in intercourse with the husband, and the excruciating sufferings imposed on her during every childbirth. The memories of all these ordeals increase the disturbance of her mental condition. Thus, it is no exaggeration to say that circumcision leads to both physical and psychological sexual trauma.

Dr. Baashir has described several case histories of psychiatric disturbances associated with the circumcision of women, such as anxiety states, psychotic excitement, reactive depressive states, etc. He clearly reported that this custom in itself constitutes important mental health problems.

Other authors have confirmed that female circumcision leads to various types of psycho-sexual aberrations. Such complications are indicated in excessive sexual taboos, sexual frigidity, pain and sufferings during the sexual act. The result of these consequences may also lead to marital difficulties and family disunity.

Notes

1. The name is associated with the origins of the practice because it is believed that it started in Ancient Egypt where virgins had to be regularly sacrificed to the gods. In order to be sure they were virgins, they had to undergo the Pharaonic operation. [Ismail, 1977:2].
2. Catgut is obtained from animal (sheep) intestines. It is dried and used as strings or thread to suture the raw edges of the wound.
3. The peoples in Africa who perform clitoridectomy after marriage, or soon after giving birth to the first child, are said to believe that the operation aids fertility and prevents sterility as well as infantile mortality. They believe that circumcision enlarges the vagina and makes child-bearing easier.
4. See also Hosken Report, 'Female Sexual Mutilations: The Facts and Proposals for Action', the *Geographical Review of Female Circumcision in the World Today* [1979:19].
5. We shall see later that education has had hardly any impact on changing this custom.
6. No social-historical analysis of the emergence of the practice of the circumcision of women among the African tribes seems to exist, therefore, at present, it is not possible for me to assess

the role of this practice vis-a-vis earlier customs.

7. Most of the information in this section is cited from an up-to-date geographical survey by Fran Hosken [Hosken, 1979]. who extensively investigated the subject and studied the custom and its distribution by reviewing the relevant medical and anthropological literature, as well as visiting most of the countries where this custom is practised.
8. The amount of tissues removed and the subsequent damage to the child depends on the skill and experience of the midwife.
9. If everything goes normally, the wound is considered to be healed and the binder is released from the girl's legs within two weeks. After healing the wound shows the labia majora meeting in the midline in a clean scar about a quarter of an inch wide. A complete occlusion of the introitus is shown except for a circular opening into the vagina, only large enough to admit the tip of the little finger. [Melly, 1930:1272).
10. Keloid formation is a sequel of circumcision which medically, is believed to be especially common after infection. [Shandall; Verzin; Modawi].
11. Research on 'Female Circumcision and Sexual Desire' was carried out in Ain Shamis University Hospital of Gynaecology and Obstetrics, Cairo by two Egyptian doctors, Mohamoud Karim and Roshdi Ammar in 1965.
12. The second research 'Circumcision and Infibulation of Females', is a very comprehensive study and was carried out in Khartoum (Sudan) General Hospital and out-patients department by Dr. Ahmed Abu-el-Futuh Shandall, of the Faculty of Medicine, University of Khartoum.

2. The Custom and Its Ideology

Official Ideology and Historical Background

To understand the Somali woman's aspirations, her struggle against out-moded social customs, and her subordinate status in society, one must know her background. Her attitude towards life, her beliefs and her values are all linked with her historical and cultural heritage. Her religion, Islam, which has governed her life for decades, is an integral part of her everyday life upon which the moral code for her personal behaviour is based.

Although nomadism is the predominant mode of life in Somali society, and nomads usually ignore some orthodox customs, exhibiting a posture of pride and independence, religion still has a vital influence on the social institutions.

Somali society in general supports the view of Islamic norms and Koranic ethics, particularly in matters relating to women's 'modesty' and social behaviour. Briefly, the term 'modesty code' in this context refers to a cluster of characteristic traits and institutions associated with women's sexuality and family honour, applicable almost throughout north-east Africa and the Middle East. These features are concerned with chastity before and after marriage, fidelity, purity, seclusion and veiling, genital mutilation, virginity, marriage, polygamy, divorce and the legitimacy of children.

As the personality and behaviour of these Muslim women is considered to be shaped from two points of view, i.e., that of the Shari'a (the Koran), and that of tribal customs and beliefs, a brief historical review of the Koran may help the reader to understand the setting within which the central theme of this book is placed.

The emergence of Islam in the 7th Century AD was a reaction to the paradoxes of its time. In pre-Islamic Arabia, where poverty and wars predominated, the Koranic pronouncements regarding social relations and the status of women can be seen as revolutionary. It is said that in pre-Islamic times, the Arabs were a male centred tribal people, who practised polygamy and kept women in inferior positions, with very limited rights and individual status. In fact, they were regarded as the most pathetic group in society. Other scholars say that in different tribes and regions women had varied marriage customs and different degrees of status within the family, some of which became less free through Islamic law. [Beck and Keddie, 1978].

There is no doubt that by and large Islam had improved the position of women in contrast to pre-Islamic times; it gave them more rights than they had previously had in some of the patriarchal tribes. Infanticide[1] was prohibited; the practice of polygamy, which had permitted any number of wives, was regulated and limited to four legal wives, with strict conditions as stated in Sura 4:3 — 'Many women of your choice, two, three or four: but if you fear you shall not be able to deal justly (with them) then only one.' Systematic, social and legal institutions were set up for matters relating to family law (marriage, divorce, inheritance, children's custody etc.). Women were given the right of inheritance for the first time, and also granted the responsibility to manage their *own* wealth, personal jewellery and to their own earnings or income.

Thus, in the domain of women's rights as in other areas of social life, the Koran served to resolve many conflicting ideas and tendencies within the society of its time which were the manifestations of the ideology of the different societies and their culture. The Koran exhorted modesty for both sexes and recognized the equality of women and men as human beings, in the spiritual and religious sphere of life at least. These principles are embodied in the following verses of the Koran:

> O mankind! Be careful of your duty to your Lord, who created you from a single soul and from it created its mate and from them twain have spread abroad a multitude of men and women. [Sura, 4:1].

And, as evidenced by the promise of equal reward, thus:

> Who ever does good works, men and women, and is a believer — we shall make them live a good life, and we shall give them

their reward for the best that they have done. [Sura, 16:99].

These two passages indicate a theoretical equality between men and women inherent in Islamic principles. During the Prophet Mohamed's time, knowledge and education were regarded as necessary for all believers, and it was regarded as incumbent upon every Muslim man and woman to seek learning. Women also used to pray in public mosques. After the death of the Prophet, however, women were prevented. Learning and scholarship were regarded as appropriate only for men; in addition, women were prevented from prayer in public mosques by the orthodox learned men, who regarded it as a threat to the seclusion system. Today, the incidence of Muslim women's public prayer varies from country to country but in any case, is insignificant.

Apart from the Koran, a second source, i.e., the *Sunna* influenced the development of the *Shari'a*. The *Sunna* are a set of traditions derived from the words and acts of the Prophet Mohamed and have undergone changes over a long period of time. The Sunni or Orthodox Muslims, who comprise most of the Arab world including the Somalis, recognize four schools of jurisprudence: the Shafis, Malikis, Hanfis and Hanbalists.

The Shia's, representing groups who dissent from the Sunni, are more independent in their interpretation of the Koran. Thus, generalization about Islamic law, particularly of personal and family law, is subject to qualifications within the Muslim world.

The legal aspects of women's status within Islam generally is a most striking example of this socio-theological order. Compared with the other major religions (Christianity, Judaism, Hinduism, or Buddhism) it is regarded by many scholars as unique. Its uniqueness lies in the degree to which these matters have been legalized either by the Koran or by subsequent legislation derived from the interpretation of the Koran and the Sunna. The Islamic Shari'a determines the rights and obligations of women in that:
1) Girls are in the custody of their fathers until they marry, at which time their husbands take over their responsibility and the women are placed under their tutelage.
2) Polygamy is only allowed for men and they are permitted to have four wives at the same time, so long as they are able to pay the bride-price for each wife and that they treat all of them equally.
3) Divorce is the privilege of men alone. The wife has the right to divorce only in exceptional cases, such as maltreatment by the

husband or if he cannot fulfil his responsibility for her physical well-being etc. Even for these cases women less frequently go to courts to reinforce their limited rights.

4) A wife's rights to the family property are unequal to that of the husband and she must have his consent to dispose of it.

5) The wife's share in inheritance varies from *one-eighth* to *one-sixteenth* of the property left by the husband (depending upon whether or not she has children).

6) The shares of the men's inheritance are twice as large as a woman's.

7) The testimony of two women witnesses equals that of one man and the penalty for killing a woman is only half that for killing a man.

8) Muslim men can marry not only Muslim women, but also women who belong to the peoples of the 'Book', (Jews and Christians). But Muslim women are allowed to marry only Muslim men.

9) Obedience of women to men, and to the canons of proper dress and modesty in their behaviour are also enshrined in the Shari'a.

10) Child custody, after a certain age that varies according to the different legal schools of thought, goes to the father.

Within points one to ten, it appears that the result still remains unequal; however, Islam maintains that since absolute equality is never possible in all situations, basic equality remains in all man-woman relations. In addition, there are other customs reinforcing male domination[2] which are widely interpreted as *Islamic* and *religious*, but supported by no specific Islamic text.

With the spread of Islam through the conquest of territories in the Middle and Near East, the development of a body of Islamic law derived from the Koran also embraced non-Islamic traditions, values, and practices which affected the status of women, including their seclusion and circumcision.

Furthermore, the Prophet Mohamed did not dispense with the general attitude which had previously relegated women to a secondary place in society.[3] In fact, the Koran reinforced this attitude in verses such as:

> Men have authority over women because Allah has made the one superior to the other, and because they spend their wealth to maintain them. [Sura, 4:34].

> Women shall with justice have rights similar to those exercised against them, although men have a status above women. Allah

is mighty and wise. [2:228, 229].

These Koranic verses were used by men to justify many more practices and serve more purposes with regard to women than was probably intended by the Koran. Also, Islam's beliefs enshrined certain customs and attitudes that resulted in establishing constraints on the freedom of women and limiting their efforts towards the achievement of equal status. For example, the inferiority of women is manifested in the practice of the Muslim religion in that women are the subjects of more states of ritual impurity than men. According to the Koran, six acts are considered to be of major ritual impurity for which Islamic legislation prescribes ablution. They are: 1) effusion of semen; 2) the blood produced after birth; 3) sexual intercourse; 4) menstruation; 5) childbirth, and 6) death. Out of these acts only one (effusion of semen) applies specifically to men, while three apply specifically to women and the remaining two (sexual intercourse and death) are shared between the sexes. During menstruation and for 40 days after childbirth, a woman is forbidden to enter any holy place. During these periods she may not have sexual intercourse, or pray, or fast during the month of Ramadan because she is considered unclean and impure. This ascription of female impurity at these times is not only found in the beliefs of other patriarchal religions — Judaism, Hinduism, Christianity — but probably has pagan roots and in many rural areas of Europe persists even today, but mainly amongst older people.

This concept of impurity had an economic motive, in that the differential values placed upon men and women determined monetary equivalents for the *vows* of persons for cult services. According to this reckoning the vow of a man aged 20 to 60 years was valued at 50 shekels,[4] while that of a woman in the same age range was worth only 30 shekels.

Thus, it appears that a male of any age was more highly valued than a female. Therefore, the reason for this differential valuation was to a large extent economically motivated rather than based on morality or psychological factors. [R.R. Ruether, 1974:54].

From this, we can also see that women suffered religious restrictions which were indirectly sex-determined and economically motivated. This was an ancient practice which the Israelite religion inherited and which subsequently was adopted by the Muslim religion. The main purpose was to exclude from cultic participation all persons in a state of impurity or uncleanness, that is, those in a 'profane' or 'unholy' state. During the impure period, it was considered unsafe to engage in religious activities or have contact with 'holy' things or places. Clearly, women suffered most from these laws, because of the period of 'impurity' during childbirth and menstruation. As we can see, this is an explicitly discriminatory usage of the natural functions of women which became conceptualized as ritual pollution.

The Traditional Muslim View of Women's Sexuality

Despite these formal religious practices in respect of women, the practice of female circumcision has no religious basis and it has been proven that the custom has a pre-Islamic origin. [Remondino, 1891; Ploss, 1885]. However, as already noted, the practice spread and gained its strength through the rise of such Islamic traditions as the veil. This is not only that some 'Ahadith' (sayings of the Prophet) are in favour of the so-called 'Sunna' type of circumcision, but it is also because Islam regards female sexuality as active and as a lustful instinct which consequently must be controlled. As a consequence great value was placed on women's modesty and chastity. Thus, although female circumcision is not mentioned in the Koran and was not an exclusively Islamic institution, it probably became more widespread in Islamic areas than elsewhere. Not all Muslims, however, practice female circumcision and infibulation e.g. it is not practised among many Arab or Indian Muslims.

It is reasonable to state that Muslim men generally seem to share similar chauvinistic attitudes towards women and the men's view is that women's sexuality is dangerous and needs to be curtailed. The Koran sees sex as one of the instincts, and stipulates that sexual enjoyment must have legal bounds (marriage); tribal customs express their fear and anxiety of women's sexuality in the concepts of 'shame and honour', which extend outside Islam. The chastity of the woman represents the honour[5] of the family, and any violation must be punished; the ultimate sanction sometimes is death to the woman, carried out by a male relative. In some countries such as Somalia, Sudan and Egypt precautionary measures take the form of female circumcision and infibulation, which can be seen as representing another extreme version of the 'honour and shame code'. The custom of veiling and seclusion, strictly observed in most of the Muslim world, is another facet of this code.

Circumcision and infibulation of women is practised only by *some* Muslim societies; especially among the nomadic tribes and the peasants who do not adhere rigidly to the custom of social segregation of the sexes. On the other hand, strict veiling and seclusion became common practices in urban areas and were traditionally limited to the upper and middle classes. Furthermore, during the era of Abbasid's rule in the 7th to 11th Centuries, the veil became a symbol of prestige and class status, being forbidden to the lower classes and to the slaves invading the market place at that time. Thus, initially the role of the veil and the seclusion of women was to protect 'family honour', and to distinguish nobility from the commoners.

The veil[6] also gained support by distinguishing women believers (i.e., the wives of the Prophet) from other women. Besides, since women were considered to be 'destructive elements', they were to be covered, confined and excluded from matters other than those of the family, and from men other than close kinsmen. Exhortations to modesty and chastity were, therefore, directed towards all believing women. Women could only adorn themselves in the presence of men whose relationship was restricted by the incest taboo, or for males disqualified as sexual objects by age (children and the old). The Koranic verses affirm this as follows:

> O Prophet speak to thy wives and to thy daughters and to the wives of the faithful, to turn their eyes away from temptation and to preserve the chastity, to cover their adornment (except such as are normally displayed); to draw their veils over their bosoms and not to reveal their finery except to their husbands, or fathers, or sons, or husband's fathers, or their step-sons, or their brothers, or their brother's sons or sister's sons, or their women, or their slaves or male attendants *who lack natural vigour*, or children who have no carnal knowledge of women's nakedness. And let them not stamp their feet in walking so as to reveal their hidden trinkets. [24:31]. (Author's emphasis).

150 years after the death of the Prophet, the veil and seclusion were well established and gradually came to be associated with the inferior position of women, increasing and legitimizing the power of men over women. Among the richer classes, it went so far as to exclude women from the rest of the household under

the charge of eunuchs. Some scholars believe that this was also a result of the early influence of the Persian interpreters of the Koran in whose country seclusion had long been practised. Hence, local practices and social divisions separated men and women even more than the Koran might have intended. This general social segregation of the sexes has helped to maintain two different societies, one of men and one of women, in most Muslim countries.

Some religions, such as Christianity, have taught that sexual activity is essentially evil, and that 'spiritual' progress is possible only through practising celibacy and monasticism; while marriage is necessary for the continuation of the family it is referred to by St. Paul as almost a last resort for those who are not able to live alone.

The Koran reflects that view; it regards the sexual impulse as a natural appetite to be gratified, albeit in moderation and under certain conditions. Islam has a very positive attitude to sexual activity for both men and women which is accompanied by a strict insistence on fidelity and chastity. Any extra-marital sexual activity is forbidden to men as well as women; suspicion of any pre-marital sexual activity, as well as of marital infidelity — whether or not confirmed — invites retribution, including divorce.

The Shari'a has shaped the legal and ideological history of the Muslim family structure and consequently of the relations between the sexes. In practice then sexual equality is seen as a violation of Islamic laws, and therefore, Islamic ideology as applied to women's position in the social order has evolved the edict that they should submit to the authority of fathers, brothers or husbands.

> Good women are obedient. They guard their unseen parts because Allah has guarded them. As for those from who you fear disobedience, admonish them and send them to beds apart and beat them. Then if they obey you, take no further action against them. Allah is high, supreme. [Sura, 4:34].

In the above quotation, the link is clearly made between ideological, legal and direct violent oppression of women by men. As expressed in the above verses, if women do not 'obey', violence is recommended to subdue them. Hence, the axiom of the natural superiority of men, which is made to justify their legal, social and economic prerogatives, is still maintained and legalized in Muslim countries.

In order to perpetuate male domination and to limit women's

fitna (or 'chaos'), women were relegated to a submissive role by giving them a negative concept of themselves which takes many forms, i.e., chastity, sexual repression, seclusion, female circumcision, polygamy (for men), monogamy (for women), motherhood and so on.

From these few examples of the traditional Islamic values, we can see that the basis of existing inequality and inferiority of women does not, in the main, rest on religious ideology as interpreted by men, but is the outcome of specific social institutions designed to limit women's sexual, social, economic, and political rights. In this way, they remain exploited. The sexual exploitation of women indeed, requires their isolation, as well as the propagation of cultural myths which reinforce a male-dominated social and political order.

In addition, the belief that women have a limited capacity for right conduct stems from other religious sources. Most patriarchal religions share this belief that women's sexuality is to be feared and, therefore, persecute, isolate and damn them. The Koran attributed powers of witchcraft to women (113–4) and in the story of the temptation of Joseph, stressed the voluptuous aspects of their character [Antoun, 1968:674]. Even today, among the religious leaders and some other fanatic traditional men and women in my society, women are regarded as more disposed to passion and emotions than to reason, and it is argued that women should be eliminated from public life *because* of their feminine attributes and an allegedly lesser capacity for vigilance, faithfulness, intelligent action and rational conduct.

There are many cautionary tales about the sexual danger of women in Muslim ethics and literature. There are examples which the Prophet delivered to believers. Such as:

> How will it be when your women become unfaithful and insolent and your men have become depraved and yourselves have departed from the struggle in the way of God?' The prophet's companion asked 'Will this come to pass, oh messenger of God?' He [the Prophet] replied, 'Yes and worse than that.' He said: 'How will it be when you no longer command the good and refrain from evil?' They asked, 'Will this come to pass oh messenger of God?' He replied, 'Yes, and worse than that.' The companions asked 'But what can be worse than that, Oh Prophet?' He said, 'How will it be when you command the evil and refrain

> from the good?' They asked, 'Will this come to pass Oh Prophet?' He replied, 'Yes by whose spirit is in my hand, God, the most high says, "Verily I shall send down upon them discord ['*fitna*'] so that the most for bearing them will be perplexed". Oh ye people, verily women are discord.' And the messenger of God did not point out to us anything more disturbing of the peace than women. The messenger of God also said 'The woman is exposed to shame, for if she leaves the house, "Satan" seeks her out and gains possession of her honour. And the woman who remains close to God, the exalted, is the woman remaining in her home.' The Prophet also told to his believers, 'There are three who will never enter the heaven: the "*dayyuth*", the *rajulata* among women and the drunkard.' The companions asked: 'Of the drinker of wine we understand, but what is the "Dayyuth"?' The Prophet said: 'It is he who does not grow angry when strangers enter upon his woman.' They asked, 'And who is the rajulata among women?' He said, 'It is the woman who seeks to dress and act like a man.'

In consideration of all this presumed danger of destruction brought about by women, the separation of the sexes is strictly observed in Muslim societies. Women are confined in their traditional roles in the house and family, and in no case are they to assert themselves as equal to 'men' (*rajul* in Arabic). As indicated in the message, a woman who shows any masculine[7] characteristic, physically or intellectually, is considered to be an outrageous and perverted creature, who has committed a sinful act that prevents her from entering heaven.

The questions to be faced here are: 1) Why is women's sexuality threatened? Why must it be controlled? 2) If men cannot cope with the sexuality of women then from what are they protecting them? Is it to be assumed that men 'protect' women from their alleged inherent 'evil' and, at the same time themselves from contamination by this 'evil'? 3) If men are so vulnerable to feminine influence perhaps *they* should be protected and veiled?

As Faduma Mernissi cited in her book *Beyond the Veil* (1975:4):

> Muslim society is characterized by a contradiction between what can be called 'an explicit theory', and an implicit theory of female sexuality and therefore a double theory of 'sexes' dynamic . . . The explicit theory is the prevailing

> contemporary belief according to which men are aggressive in their interaction with women, and women are passive. The implicit theory is epitomized in Iman Gazali's classical work. He sees civilization as struggling to contain the women's destructive, all absorbing power. Women must be controlled to prevent men from being distracted from their social and religious duties.

Ghazali's concept of female sexuality is that of the Muslim societies which regard *female sexuality as 'active'*; this was quite the opposite of the 'bourgeois' concept[8] of women's sexuality as '*passive*'; a concept 'scientifically' reinforced by a superficial interpretation of Freudian theories. Nevertheless, what is interesting here is that both theories come to the same conclusion. Both theories describe women as 'destructive elements' to the social order, i.e. civilization. Both societies feel threatened by women although they put forward two different reasons.

In this context, different masculine views have interpreted the tensions between religion and sexuality in different ways. In Islam, men see women as the symbol of disorder and *fitna*,[9] therefore, the virtue of the woman, namely the fulfilment of her sexual needs by her husband inside marriage, which prevents *Zina* (illicit relationships, adultery and fornication) is a guarantee of the maintenance of the patriarchal order.

Whilst being aware that the theories of Marx and Engels were developed at a specific historical moment in Western European society, it is perhaps not unreasonable to see this contradiction in terms of the outcome of the form of property and the social relations of production. Suggestive too, of how the present condition of women resulted from the historical development of the institution of private property, the state and the family — how men have developed their potentialities at the expense of women and how this is related to the development of the ruling classes at the expense of the masses. That is, with the advent of private property, the concept of ownership was extended to include slaves and women as the private property of men.

Accumulation of what we now perceive of as private property, and passing this on to the sons, was an important feature of the patriarchal family and lineage. The need for sexual purity of women was integrated into this system because the patriarchal family was deeply concerned to establish means to ensure that family wealth passed only to the *legitimate* heirs. Consequently, the sexual ideology, whereby women's sexual freedom had to be strictly controlled, was reinforced. Thus, any encounter between the sexes outside of those specifically sanctioned was seen as a threat to the social order. To maintain this system, therefore, the women and their children were subject to institutions to legitimize male dominance; a process further consolidated by interpretations (by men) of religious teachings.

In conclusion, to summarize our understanding: fear of women's sexuality led men into imposing upon them strict control — purdah — eliminating them from public, social and economic spheres, and demanding their virginity and chastity. This, in many societies, entails clitoridectomy and infibulation, all in order to control the bodies of women as the means of reproduction, and to serve as an impediment to their sexual power. Both are obtained by violence and socio-economic rewards and punishment, and further reinforced by the existing exploitative social order.

Significance of Circumcision Within the Somali Value System

If we are to understand the strength of any belief in any culture, it is necessary to examine how it fits into the total structure of that society. My purpose here is, then, to examine and explain the significance of female circumcision within Somali culture, how it fits into the social system, and the system of values — mainly inherited from Islam and other Middle Eastern cultures — it embraces.

It is important to note here that the custom of infibulation is seen as having a positive function with respect to other components of the patriarchal Somali familial practices (such as marriage, the modesty code, family honour, women's social roles and life patterns, and the patrilineage) which are fundamental to Somali society.

The infibulation practised in Somalia seems to be a socio-cultural feature of almost the entire area referred to as North-East Africa. It is practised in Somalia, Jibouti, Eritrea, Sudan, Egypt and to some extent in Ethiopia. [Shandall, 1967:178]. In these countries, the social groups which practice infibulation have different economic systems, political organizations, marriage practices and languages. However, along with the custom of infibulation, Somalia shares with these cultural groups a commitment to Islamic ideology (with the exception of parts of Ethiopia) and they are all traditionally patrilineal, patrilocal, and patriarchal societies. Thus, to fully understand the traditional status of Somali women consideration must be given to the religious ordinances enumerated previously.

That Somali society is experiencing a period of transition in which the old and the new exist side by side must also be borne in mind. The age-old customs and attitudes rooted in an ancient and venerable culture have acted to partially impede the transformation process. While the urban groups are making rapid changes and transformations are possible, the rural groups and tribal nomads have remained relatively poor and tradition bound. Many religious leaders have generally supported the changes but many continue to adhere to the old customs, and to consider 'modernization' and Western culture as a threat to Muslim order and their authority.

The Nomad Social Structure and Value System

Somalia is a country with a pastoral nomadic society. Almost 80% of the population live in the rural areas where survival is demanding and hard. In those regions far from rivers, the grass that springs up during the rainy seasons provides grazing for large herds of camels, cattle, sheep and goats. Animal husbandry is, therefore, the economic basis of an independent nomadic mode of life in which subsistence depends primarily upon milk and other animal products. Around those areas primarily in the flood plains, and irrigated areas near the Juba and Shebelle rivers and in the north-west region, agricultural production is divided equally between animal husbandry and growing crops, mainly millet, sesame, bananas, sugar cane, grapefruit and mango.

The nomads migrate with the seasonal cycles because of their marginal environment, and the consequent need to find sufficient food and water for their stock. The nomadic value system is all-embracing and clearly defined, and draws its content from nomadic tradition and the mainstream of Islamic beliefs. To the nomad everything in the world around him functions in accordance with God's will. The prophecies, and conformity with the tenets of Islam, constitute the other pillar of influence upon which their value system rests. Religious men, *Wadaad*, play a vital role among the nomads: they treat the sick, and initiate the rituals associated with the young, and ceremonies and feasts of birth, marriage and death. They have taught in Koranic schools, where many Somalis have obtained their only formal education.

The Family

The primary social unit is the immediate family 'Qoys'[10] or 'Reer', consisting of father, mother and children, and, unlike the nuclear family, extending to the blood relatives of both spouses.

Since the Somalis trace their descent through the male, the term 'Reer' refers not only to the immediate family, but also applies to the man's family and most distant relatives. Somali political organizations are based on kinship, thus, an aggregate of families inter-related and bound together by blood, live, travel, camp and go to war together. In other words, the 'Reer', composed of lineage or alliance of lineages, share the same properties as kinship groups.

Great importance is attached to the tribe, the clan, to the big family with many sons, and to communal thinking. With frequent local disputes over land, water, women, invaders and other rights, it is essential for each family and lineage to be as large and as strong as possible, and its strength is very much dependent upon the number of sons.

Male superiority is intricately woven into customs and Islamic traditions. Since the Somalis are patrilineal the nomadic lifestyle is suited to the conveniences of the men. Women are dependent on a traditional division of labour which is heavily biased against them. The father is head of the family, and the ultimate arbitrator and controller of family property. The woman has no legal identity in the strict sense of the word. Her property and assets are handled by the male head of the family, whether father, brother or husband. Women are considered to be intellectually inferior to men.

From an early age the Somali boys are trained to adopt a fundamentally masculine culture; a socialization system which girls and women are not permitted to share.

The ideal picture of a man, which Somalis refer to as *nin ragah* (a *real* man) is seen as strong, courageous, proud, assertive, reliable, resourceful, honourable, daring (willing to take risks), warm, generous, firm, outspoken and poetic.

As in many other societies, the ideal woman is seen as able, possessed of initiative, strong — but with the strength of a 'feminine' type, i.e. she must not try to assume masculine attributes and, most importantly, she must in no way challenge men's authority. Her strength must be of a kind capable of concealing her man's weaknesses.

Women's Role in the Family

The educated and privileged classes in urban areas obviously differ from the simple, nomadic and peasant women, and although no generalized picture of women in society is possible the basic traditional concepts of their role are similar.

A woman is traditionally considered to be the backbone of the family in all classes of the society. It is her responsibility to keep the house and bring up the children. The social position of a family is usually determined by that of the husband, but it is widely held that a family is mainly what the wife makes of it. Despite this, the influential position of the wòman in the Somali family is not always apparent. Women, especially nomadic women in Somalia, bear a heavy burden with no recognized prestige; a fact of which she herself is not conscious. In general, nomadic women play a bigger part in the life of their communities than do the men.

Nomadic women care for numerous livestock; they process pastoral products such as milk, cream, 'ghee' (butter); weave mats, rugs and make other handicrafts for the Somali mobile hut (*Guri*); they dismantle and build the hut and make all the household utensils out of local materials. They fetch water and firewood (which is regarded almost exclusively as a woman's task) no matter how far they may have to go to get them. What is left for the men are tasks associated with tribal leaders and the sedentary community and caring for the herds. Men also tend and milk camels, because they consider it a strong, tough animal which women are not physically equipped to deal with. Camels are a capital resource and a highly desirable form of wealth among the Somalis.

In the urban areas, the majority of lower middle class women are busy all day working around the house, preparing food and attending to their children. Since she cannot afford modern household conveniences, the domestic routine absorbs practically all her time, while the husband is trying to earn enough to maintain the children and his non-earning housewife. She rarely participates in discussions on general issues of the society, because she has no spare time to take part. Women, in general, never go to cafes, which are the scene of social and political gatherings of men in the urban areas and the villages.

In nomadic communities men have their *shir* (meetings) within the *ardea* (fence of the compound) or under the trees; women never go near these places; they cook and serve the men behind the scenes. Women usually serve the best parts of the food to the men of the family, whilst the women, regardless of age, eat separately after the men. For these women, socializing and entertainment is confined to special occasions, such as weddings, funerals, alms-giving functions and other public religious festivities.

The position of middle class and educated women in the family has steadily improved since Somalia's Independence in 1960. These women are becoming relatively more emancipated compared to rural and poorer groups of women. The middle class family is able to buy some modern electrical appliances as well as to employ servants (exploiting other women) thus releasing middle class women from the drudgery of housework and child care. This enables them to spend more time pursuing other interests, such as studying and/or working outside the home.

In spite of this, the birth of a boy is still considered good fortune, while that of a girl is met with less enthusiasm. A girl's conduct might bring disgrace to the family honour; girls do not increase the lineage population or carry the family name, even though they do bring in wealth.

A contradictory feature of women's position in the family is the belief that without their generous heart, patience, sense of responsibility, hard work and awareness of kinship, the system would not have survived. She is expected to provide wider services to all the extended family members, as this type of family is both a social and judicial family. Yet, she is dominated by the man. The explanation seems to lie in the social institutions, patterns of the patriarchal social order, and on the need of the man for a woman to bear him sons.

Apart from her ties to her children, to enjoy better economic security and safeguard her livelihood, a typical Somali woman is expected to constantly display an attitude of tenderness, spontaneous self-denial and self-sacrifice, not only towards her family, but also towards the whole tribe or clan of her husband. The following poem describes the ideal wife of the 'egalitarian' Somali society. A husband's advice to a newly wed young wife, given in the form of a Gabay (poem):

Ideal Wife

Both among the noble Isahhaag and Maalinguir clans,
(As well as among) the Abasguul, Bartire, Reer
Garaad, and reer Kooshin' groups.
(And also among) the Ararasame, and the Iidoor of
the country around Oodweyne.
Through the Uubaale and Adari countries, as well as
Iimay.
(And Also) at Ilig, Aware and Jeed (not to mention)
at the wells of CeelDhinle.
In the towns and at Buhodle,
Lo, among the entire inhabitants of the four direc-
tions —
In all these places, (and among all these people) I
searched for a (good) wife.
If, oh, my green one, I chose you as a wife,
And ignored all the others, selecting you for your
noble birth,
(Then listen to me) like a pupil to his teacher,
(Oh my fair one), give heed to my advice, for I
shall enlighten you.

The wife of a husband of low birth never smells
well, for she never burns incense for herself.
After she gives birth, she becomes even worse, and
her husband abandons her.
(Therefore), be generous with water to your body
and soul.
(My clan) despises a women (covered) with dirt; so
you should never allow it to collect on yourself.
I am a man who appreciates (sweet) smelling things,
(so) do not shrink (from the use of (incense);
As long as you remain with me never cease to use
the incense burner.

If a girl is married into my clan, they always
check her background,
(Take heed!) Their methods include arrogance and
ridicule, which is intended to tame the girl.
(Therefore), clean your mouth and teeth, and always
use your eyeshadow,
One should never find you untidy.

(It is shameful) for the inside of your ante-chamber or the area around it,
To become disorderly, as though it were a thorny camel-corral,
(Therefore), take care that it does not resemble (such a place) — it should be cozy and neat.
(My) bed-chamber should be especially tidy.
Yet the inside must be large enough for guests.

Never ignore my cousins and those of my kind and relations
Who might come to visit when I am present,
(Let it be unnecessary) for me to tell you my thoughts,
Understand them, for a good wife is always sensitive.

(A group of noble men) may appear at dusk —
(Remember that) the clans from the west never sit in unclean places;
(Such as) at the gate of the corral;
My clan, the Reer-Ugaas-Magan, are too noble for such places.
They do not resemble other people, so you should never ignore them as though they were common.
Learn their ways from this time forth!
Having clad yourself fully —
(Never forgetting) the four earrings and the amulets you have with you in the house —
Go to them and meet the (noble men) of the Ba-Hhawaadle.
During my absence, if relatives come to you as guests,
Never turn them away uncared for;
News of your neglect should never reach my ears.
Such people should never complain to me for not having been (properly) fed (in my house).
Always care for the aged (and the needy) for generosity is a quality of a good wife.

(The wife) who always nags is like the satan (himself)
Always be sensitive, walk prudently and speak slowly.

Take care of your manner (and) watch your language,
for decency is noble.

If I should punish you for wrong-doing,
(Take care that) you conceal your feelings, (for
this) is wiser than weeping.
(For only) a bad wife exhibits her grievance:
Beware that other people should behold your crying.

Thus I speak to you as a warning and as advice,
If Allah make you understand (what I give you) is a
complete book (of advice)
If, (on the other hand) you ignore all these good
counsels,
(Then no matter) who else Allah might give you as a
husband,
We two will (have to) separate.

(Extracted from an article on 'Somali Traditional Marriage'
by Musa Galaal, 1968).

These verses clearly illustrate what is seen as an ideal personality for a woman in our society. The importance of family and lineage ties as a part and parcel of a patrilineal clan system under which the Somalis live becomes very evident here. The poem also demonstrates — in a country where masculine pride is paramount and men readily proclaim and assert their superiority over women — paradoxically women's role in the family is so important.

The traditional women take all these beliefs and customs for granted and exhibit a curious mixture of humility and dignity and in no way consider themselves to be oppressed. In fact, they often greatly influence the men of their families in a quite unobtrusive way and are generally cherished and loved by all the male members of the lineage.

Sex Norms and Attitudes

Purdah[11] is practically unknown among Somali women in rural areas, because of the harsh climatic and other natural conditions and her vital role in nomadic society. Because of this basic nomadic tradition, purdah has never been compulsory in urban communities. The relative freedom of movement of the nomads, and their less restricted way of life, permits comparatively greater interaction between the sexes, but this is limited to verbal repartee and love play, no physical contact is allowed among the unmarried youth. Any indulgence, however innocent, may ruin a girl's chance of marriage, because family and lineage ties, and virginity are of cardinal importance to the nomads, perhaps more so than any other community, although virginity is highly valued among the Somali society at large.

In general, the sex life of the women begins with marriage. Given their moral customs and religious training, approximately 90% of all Somali girls remain virgins until they marry. Perhaps inevitably, a double standard of morality accompanies these norms for women.

1) Virility is the incentive especially for urban men to seek sexual experience at an early age. For some men sexual activity is a source of pride; whereas the sexual experience of women is a source of shame and a symbol of degradation.

2) The emphasis on virginity imposes circumcision and infibulation on girls; and strict prohibitions from any kind of sexual activity before marriage. Girls who deviate from this rule are held in contempt by society because even the most liberal of men shy away from the possibility of marrying a woman with pre-marital sexual experience. If, during a couple's engagement the man learns that his fiancee has had such experience he breaks off the engagement. If the bridegroom discovers that his bride is not a virgin, he immediately sends her back to her family and demands the return of his bride-price.

3) The rules applying to matrimonial fidelity also require a woman to avoid any act that a jealous husband might regard as a threat to his sexual monopoly of her. In other words, she must carefully avoid any situation in which any man might find an opportunity to court her. Thus, in social relations there is an instinctive tendency for the sexes to separate; the women in one corner talking about children and household matters, while in another corner, the men talk about business, politics, sports and the like. The separation of the sexes is to be observed especially at gatherings occasioned be death, weddings and other ceremonies.

If a married woman is caught in or even suspected of adultery, she may be divorced and also condemned by her husband, her family and by the whole society. This is operative not only in the upper and middle, but also in the lower classes, including the poor, rural population. Failure to divorce or punish the wife results in the loss of honour and status of the husband and his clan in society.

The wives generally tolerate their husbands' extra-marital affairs, whether adulterous or polygamous; provided that they are carried on discreetly. A wife will usually resign herself to the situation rather than react vehemently; she has practically no other alternative. At the root of this discrimination lies the fact that women are pressured to be infibulated and remain virgins to protect the family honour while men are tacitly allowed sexual experience, some of them even believing that it improves their virility and feeling that it boosts their masculine pride. As Lewis points out: 'Some men even sometimes claim to deliberately restrain their sexual urges for fear of appearing too dependent on their wives.' [Lewis, 1962:III:42]. Similar behaviour by women, either within or outside marriage, is considered to be the gravest of offences.

Consequently, excision and infibulation are usually intended to reduce the sexual sensitivity and activity of women, and allegedly to please the man, whose sexual sensations seemingly are increased by the artificially contracted genital organs of the woman. In a much quoted 'hadith', the Prophet told a woman who had just been converted to Islam and was thinking of being circumcised: 'Do not inflict trouble on yourself, because that is painful to a wife, but pleasing to a husband.' It should be remembered that this pleasure for the man is paralleled in the woman by acute anxiety, frustration and revulsion. In studying the cases of revulsion among circumcised women, Karim and Ammar interviewed 200 circumcised women, of whom 88 experienced revulsion in one form or another. [Karim and Ammar, 1965: 121;23]. There is also the psychological implication that women should not compete with dominant, masculine sexual performance, and by extension, they should accept male superiority in all other activities as well.

In this connection, it is relevant to note that the Koran does not cite the manifest function of circumcision to be only to ensure virginity; it is also linked to the prevention of independent sexual pleasure and excitability of women. This is based on physiological grounds, because potentially the key function of the clitoris seems to be to provide sexual pleasure for women and has no direct procreative utility. But since the main interest of the man is to father offspring whose physical, legal and ritual purity are in every way assured, the reduction of women's capacity for erotic pleasure was thus seen as necessary to enforce chastity and fidelity. In short, men's interest is solely in the organ associated with their sexual function — the vagina — which is also the canal through which their offspring come. In fact they fear the clitoris, and therefore remove it.

Infibulation is seen as an additional control of women's erotic desires, not only to maintain virtue in youth but, at the time of marriage, to assure the bridegroom that he is her first and only man.

Hence the principal effect of the operation is to create in young girls an intense awareness of her sexuality and anxiety concerning its meaning, its social significance. In general, the practice emphasizes punishment and social control, clearly indicating to the little girl a sense of the mystery and importance of sex, and, at the same time creating a fear of the evils of unchaste behaviour in her.

The painful operation and its complications are usually camouflaged by earlier psycho-social customs related to the marriage systems, the role of the bride, the bride-price, the norms of sexual behaviour and the responsibility for maintaining family honour.[12] It is assumed that she will accept and act in accordance with these values for the sake of her family and lineage, etc.

Long before the actual operation, the little girl is likely to hear about it. As she grows up within the context of her cultural norms, she becomes familiar with the assumption that an uncircumcised girl is unacceptable, and that no one will marry a women who is not circumcised. Gradually, her psycho-social community traits develop and her attitude of mind and general behaviour are shaped accordingly. Therefore, every little girl looks forward to her purification (in Somali — *xalaalays*).

In urban areas, a girl's appearance in public is more restricted after puberty; she is closely supervised. Girls are considered to be of marriageable age when they are about 15 years old. They are extremely worried about their reputation and consequently are unlikely to succumb sexually to anyone; they must be exceedingly careful to avoid becoming the object of gossip. Repeated dating with one particular young man (if it happens) is interpreted as serious interest, and ordinarily, before long, it is expected that a declaration will be made through her family. If such an affair does not lead to a proposal, the girl's subsequent eligibility may be severely damaged.

The appearance of women in public has a shameful connotation. This attitude is so intense that in order to avoid censorious glances, though Somali women do not veil they wear long dresses and cover themselves with shawls or traditional colourful cloths as an additional concealment for their body and head. In the rural areas only married women cover their heads.

Illegitimate births do occur, but rarely, as women must be exceedingly careful, since birth control is not allowed and abortion is illegal and a pregnant woman who consents to it and anyone who performs it is punished. Social disapproval of pre- and extra-marital sexual experiences is demonstrated by the stigma attached to unmarried, especially middle class, mothers who engage in such practices, and to children born out of wedlock. No law protects them and society condemns them.

Prostitution has become increasingly visible in the urban areas since the Second World War. Society at large views this as a negative trend. Religious men especially, periodically wage campaigns against sexual adventures and the Government occasionally issues orders to abolish prostitution. So far, one big research project has been undertaken in this field and there were plans for the rehabilitation of prostitutes.

Although religious men see prostitution as moral depravity, they also regard it as a form of rebellion on the part of the woman. Interestingly enough, it is those women who are basically unwilling to fulfil the traditional submissive roles of wives and mothers, who usually engage in prostitution in order to survive.

Female Circumcision and the Economics of Marriage

The role of excision for an eligibly marriageable woman is a significant mark of womanhood and chastity, and highly valued in Somali society. Circumcision explicitly transforms a girl into a potentially marriageable woman. Circumcision, excision and infibulation are thus perceived as preliminary stages to marriage. The ritual of infibulation is especially important in the preparation of girls for entrance into adult status.

The Bride's Virginity

The bride's virginity is usually proved, and evidence proudly displayed on the second day following the wedding celebrations. The anxieties surrounding this occasion and its general importance are highly intensified. The bridegroom's family may examine the bride to ascertain her virginity, and only after they are satisfied that this is intact, will the marriage be consummated. A painful consequence of infibulation is the operation that must be performed to open the vagina for penetration during coitus — in most cases this is facilitated by a midwife incising the scar with a knife or razor. In some cases it is left to the groom, as a demonstration of his virility, and to dramatize the submission of the bride to his will.

In any event, for the bride, the initial nights of intercourse are inevitably, intensely painful. In addition to this suffering she is unsure what kind of behaviour to expect from her husband during private moments. She is conditioned to feel shame about sexual matters, to tolerate pain and is often frightened at the prospect of intimate contact. The fear surrounding initial intercourse is magnified by the memory of the pain and sufferings of excision and infibulation, as well as the recent, painful re-opening of the infibulation.

The husband is also traumatized to some extent, especially if he is to defibulate the bride himself and his virility is to be tested by a sexual performance with an hysterical and terrified young bride whose vagina is almost totally closed. Somehow, the bridegroom conceals his marriage trauma, asserting the image of himself as a dominant male mastering a female. By the same token, the ideal bride is submissive, and deferential to all her husband's needs and comforts.

The consummation of marriage is thus full of terror and anxiety, although these fears may be slightly counteracted by rumours that the sex act will eventually be pleasurable.

The Somali concept of virginity (based on circumcision and infibulation) and the complex behaviour pattern associated with it, influences the status assignment of the family. This concept and behaviour pattern must be maintained at all costs *even* during the phases of a woman's life which involves marital (legal) sexual intercourse.

The importance attached to the concept of virginity in Somali ideology cannot be over-emphasized. The infibulation scars are a seal attesting to the intangible but vital property of the social groups' patrimony, the honour of the family and patrilineage. This seal and a woman's sexual purity, must be transferred intact upon marriage into another lineage. Should either not be intact, the girl will be totally unacceptable to that lineage as the family involved would eschew ties with a lineage without honour. Preservation of purity and honour is thus essential if her patrilineage is to maintain its social status, broaden its kinship ties and *enhance* its patrimony. This is the economic rationale for the custom.

The traditional Somali marriage has two aspects, a union of two spouses and an alliance between two lineages. Marriage is a business transaction, a contract with assumed specific rights and obligations of the two parties. It is a major means of strengthening the clan and clan's relationship with other groups.

According to Musa Galaal in his article on 'Somali Traditional Marriage' [1968:5], in Somali legend marriage is said to be of three kinds:

1. *Dab-dab-ku-gabo*, meaning 'Add two fires together' (signifying marriage between two poor families).
2. *Badhi-dab-ku-gab* meaning 'Add fat to fire' (signifying one between a poor and a rich family).
3. *Badhi-badhi-ku-gabo*, meaning 'Add fat to fat' (signifying marriage between two rich families).

Most men like to marry women from powerful clans. A powerful clan does not signify the numerical aspect, but the quality of leadership, nobility, wealth, resourcefulness and courage. Traditionally, marriage between close kin-groups was regarded in most parts of our country as taboo. No man could marry a girl whose father was in the same *Dia*[13] (paying group) or in the same *shir* (meeting group). A Somali saying expresses that taboo in addressing a marriageable girl: '*Naa soo muude mooyiye, soo meere kuma geyo*'. Which means: 'Oh you girl, the man who comes round the fence is not your equal; the man who travels to you through danger and desolate country, like a lion, is your equal.'

So traditionally, a marriage from within a clan distant in location and genealogy is considered an important base for personal and family nobility. It means only rich clans could have such distant relations.

A Meher (Dowry)

This must be paid to the wife according to the terms of the marriage contract, and usually be comparable to that received by her mother or elder sisters before her. The dowry is the *personal property* of the wife and can be given to her during the marriage or immediately on divorce. According to Muslim law, divorce is the husband's prerogative, he may divorce his wife at will and without court proceedings. As a safeguard for women, and to provide them with some means of maintenance, Muslim law provides for a sum of wealth (in the form of money, jewellery, livestock, etc.), to be paid by the husband to his wife. The amount varies from community to community, depending on the other local customs relating to the practice of marriage.

In traditional marriage among the Somali nomadic camel herders of the north, the *Meher* may consist of up to 100 camels. This is not only because the status of women — who are regarded as productive workers — is high, but also because the alliance provided by marriage ties are of such importance that the severance occasioned by divorce requires substantial compensation. Among the agrarian and urban communities in the south who strictly apply the Islamic rate, it may be 400 shillings. In many cases, women who want a divorce usually sacrifice their *Meher* in order to gain their freedom.

Divorce is very common in Somali society, and the unequal relationship between men and women enables a man to divorce his wife for whatever reason he chooses. A woman can be divorced for failing to bear children, and sometimes for failing to bear sons. The existence of the institution of polygamy also contributes to marital instability, as it is a source of worry and insecurity for women. Those who have no co-wives are always threatened with the prospect of the husband taking an additional wife or wives.

Bride-Price

An important part of a Somali marriage is payment of the bride-price (*Yarad*, in Somali). The terms vary, but traditionally the bridegroom offers substantial bridewealth to his father-in-law.

Once a marriage proposal has been made, and before the actual wedding ceremony it is customary to give a present (*Gabaati*) to the bride's kin because, as has already been noted, traditional Somali marriage is regarded not so much as between two individuals as between two kinship groups. When asked who requested a girl in marriage, the name of her husband's lineage is usually given. Much of the bride-price could be in the form of a large number (up to 100) of camels, or a piece of land among the agrarian communities, while in urban society it usually takes the form of money, land, buildings, etc. Most people believe that the bride-price constitutes compensation to the bride's family for the loss of a working member, as well as a deterrent factor against easy divorce.

Among the nomads the bride's father returns some of the bride-price to the groom's lineage. This is called *Yarad sooran* and means that the father has equipped his daughter with all the necessary things for the new home, especially the craftwork required for the nomadic mobile house (*Guri*). It is also customary that whenever the girl returns to or visits her family, she is given a substantial gift (*dhibaad*) in the form of livestock by her father or brothers.

There is no fixed law regarding how much bride-price should be given in any marriage. This depends upon the financial situation of the bridegroom and the extent to which he values the position of the girl and her family.

The Position of the Girl

This does not always depend solely upon her beauty and tribe; consideration is also given to her background and decency. The best marriage is always based on *Hiddo-Raac*, in which the deciding factor is the decency and quality of the family background. The prospective groom may claim his right to ascertain that the girl is a virgin by inspecting the infibulation scar, because, as we said earlier, unimpeachable virginity is essential to a girl on her first marriage. For the prospective groom the virginity test is a means of confirming a woman's modesty and potential fidelity. For the family, as we have seen, incision and infibulation are the means of inculcating desirable morality, preserving modesty and guaranteeing the acquisition of a husband from a respectable family. Protecting and safeguarding the security of the patrilineage is of utmost importance; it is the basic survival unit in the hostile world outside the family circle.

The woman's social position continues to be defined in part by her membership in her father's house even after her marriage. She keeps her father's name and seeks refuge in his house from mistreatment by her husband. [Rosefield, 1966:67; Antoun, 1968: 692]. The dual loyalties of the married woman are reflected in the lineage term of address she retains. Finally, she remains part of the 'prestige' structure of her father's descent group while in addition becoming incorporated, through her children, into the 'prestige' structure of her husband's descent group. That her patrilineal kinsmen bear the major responsibility for her behaviour in any 'case of honour' demonstrates the continuing social and legal identification with her father's group. Lewis indicates that: 'Ultimately, the woman's own kin are more concerned than her husband's kin in any serious offence committed by or against her and it is they who claim her bloodwealth if she is murdered.' [Lewis, 1962:40].

In this case, a woman's immodest action before marriage threaten only her father's house, but immodest actions after marriage threaten both her father's and her husband's houses. Abou-Zeid provides a clear picture of the significance of this that is pertinent to the Somalis as well as generally for the Middle East. He writes:

> Contrary to the prevalent idea, the woman who occupies a secondary position in relation to men, is always regarded as something sacred and to be protected from desecration. In fact, much of the honour of the *beit* (family) and the lineage depends on observing this sanctity and in this sense a woman plays a vital and unique role in preserving the honour of her people. This role is connected in the first place with her nature as a female, subject to sexual desires and temptations. The reputation of a woman and her people thus depends mainly on her willingness to observe the rigid and severe rules governing sexual relationships, and on her ability to preserve her chastity. It is a most humiliating and destructive blow to the honour of the lineage if a woman is discovered to have yielded to her sexual impulses outside marriage. Thus the main contributions a woman makes to the honour of the lineage is through the passive role of preserving her chastity and purity. [Abou-Zeid, 1965].

This explanation demonstrates the societal desire that sexually, the woman must exhibit an unnatural passivity. She is not required to be sexually active, 'like an animal'. Only passive behaviour will enable her to fulfil the demand for chastity imposed on her by the two social groups to which she is responsible throughout her life.

The Social Position of Women in Somalia Today

Women's struggle to achieve equal opportunities with men began with the liberation movement for independence in the 1950s, gained momentum in the course of time, and was highlighted in the Socialist Revolution of 1969. The Somali Revolution has taken into consideration the fact that women's liberation is a basic factor for the overall struggle towards social progress and the foundation of a socialist society. For that reason, Mohamed Siad Barre, the President of the Somali Democratic Republic (S.D.R.) stated that, 'Women are a great working force which the reactionaries undermine.' (8 March 1975). Women, in spite of all their work, were considered social and economic dependants. This is still the case for the majority of working, unpaid women, especially in the rural areas where they are engaged in agricultural work and animal husbandry.

Women have no cash income of their own, nor any social or economic position distinct from that of the family; in short, their economic position is determined by the men of their family. The income generated from selling butter, small game animals, vegetables and handicraft work in semi-rural areas is, as a rule, too small to give them any economic independence. In semi-rural areas and among the lower urban class, however, women only work outside the home if serious economic circumstances make it necessary, never because of an interest in the job. Even then, their work is largely of the most menial type and contributes nothing to their social status.

Naturally, women wish to free themselves from the burden of such degrading work by making a good marriage, that is, by marrying a man whose economic status will enable them to stay at home and enjoy a better life with greater prestige. Most Somali men consider it a matter of personal honour to be able to keep their wives at home. In this position the woman is entirely dependent. She serves only her husband and produces children for him. She owns nothing, not even herself. Her children, her work and herself are all the husband's personal property to dispose of at will.

A few women are part-time specialists, such as the midwives and leaders of women's cults. These limited specializations constitute the few achieved roles available to traditional women. The ideal most often enforced, however, is that of a woman who remains in her house, catering for her family, tending the children, and taking care of the domestic livestock or working in the field if she is in an agricultural area.

In urban areas, the status of middle class women has been improved and the desire for economic independence has been awakened. The number of new jobs now available to women is a significant indication of the emerging new Somalia, and women's economic horizon has widened considerably. Economic necessity has led women into all types of employment, and paid occupations are today increasingly seen as natural for women. This has secured for women relatively better social positions compared to those who are not employed. Above all, outside employment has brought them relatively greater economic independence with all the social and class consequences this infers, including a change in status.

Apart from the stereotype women's jobs (teaching, nursing,

secretarial, etc.), a number of them are acquiring higher education and trying to advance their own professional work as doctors, lawyers, university lecturers and administrators. There are also women working in all the small industries, such as textile and food etc., and the number of women petty traders has increased significantly. Women have also joined the armed forces, the various branches of public administration (at local and central levels) and become active in political and party work.

Although, recently, a few women were promoted to become head of sections, services, and even heads of departments of ministerial services, the number of those at the higher administrative and managerial levels is still minimal. Women encounter much greater difficulties than do men in trying to obtain higher decision-making positions or to advance themselves in their work, due, primarily, to the still existing prejudice against the value of women's work.

Labour legislation gives equal rights to both sexes: 'Equal pay for equal work', but in some cases women are not given equally comparable work or positions as men, and hence are paid less. Labour law also provides for maternity leave of four months, and two hours daily breast-feeding for up to one year. The establishment of day-care centres for children has already been introduced in the big cities.

Socially conscious Somali women are struggling for the implementation of the Amendments to the family law passed in 1975. Women now at least have certain rights in matters of divorce and marriage. There are specific conditions attached to marriage involving a second, third or fourth wife. It is strictly conditioned and restricted. Marriage must be based upon mutual consent and respect, with both men and women sharing equally in family responsibilities. The bride-price and the marriage contract were placed under the jurisdiction of civil courts, the bride-price has been substantially reduced. The legal age of marriage became 18 for girls and 20 for men, and the consent of at least one parent or guardian is necessary only for those under 20 years old. Fathers cannot force their daughters into marriage. Divorce can only be obtained by judicial action. The absolute right of the man to divorce his wife as and when he pleases was abolished, both husband and wife have the right to sue for divorce.

Men and women now have equal inheritance rights, which is a very daring measure for a Muslim country to adopt. Somalia today has as modern a family code as any country in the world, but the patriarchal customs of centuries cannot be easily changed by law.

In the end, the question must be asked: why the emphasis on the modesty of women, their virginity tests, their protection and control for reasons of family honour etc? Why are excision and infibulation presented as essential in terms of the culture concerned? Why the double standards about sex and the ambivalence towards women in Somali society?

The difficulty in answering these questions is that they stem from an assumption. There is an ambivalence about sex on the part of men in most patriarchal societies. It is designed for pleasure and for producing children, yet since it is the women who serve the main reproductive function they have at least one power which men cannot entirely control. But sexuality and female reproductive functions are seen as harmful and 'impure'! This ambiguity embraces women generally, both as an extension of attitudes towards their procreative processes, and because women are at the same time makers and breakers of the family — the centre of the domestic unit, yet the potential means of disgrace and dishonour to the wider group of male kin. Here, at least in Muslim society the question of modesty in relation to women's sexuality must be considered in terms of control of reproduction, in the context of ownership and inheritance of property. If excision and infibulation are performed to limit pre- or extra-marital sex by wives and daughters, it appears from the evidence we have that this is more a concern with reproduction and with the *legality* of paternity, than of morality.

Thus, in Somalia, it appears that women are physically mutilated in order to serve certain economic and political interests of men. From the concern with paternity, it appears that the stress on family honour and the chastity of the women is due not only to the allegedly aggressive nature of women's sexuality but is closely associated with the maintenance of property and inheritance rights over women and other possessions. As such, circumcision and infibulation and the practice of chastity and fidelity have apparently risen in order to justify property relations. Women's bodies may thus be seen as a commodity or tool to be shaped, (or mutilated in this case) in any fashion that appears to be necessary to maintain this patriarchal order or property inheritance line.

This leads us to speculate that the origin of the practice is not in essence religious, but stems from an earlier economic system. Islamic religious principles which developed alongside this would naturally be interpreted in such a way as to legitimize it. Consequently, with the coming of Islam, the practice of circumcision and infibulation rooted in pre-Islamic patriarchal tribal society was reinforced by a religion based on patriarchal rule and patrilineal inheritance patterns.

Notes

1. Attitudes and customs that were current in the life of some Arab tribes, supporting the idea that the birth of a baby girl was a misfortune, and that she was better buried alive while still an infant, were invalidated and the practice forbidden under Islamic law.
2. The basic patterns of male domination such as the emphasis on virginity, fidelity, the desirability of fathering, a sexual double standard, existed in the Middle East and in other parts of the world long before Islam and are part of the patriarchal organization of many nomadic societies.
3. Patriarchal tribes' assumption of masculine superiority vis-a-vis women existed in pre-Islamic societies and was then reiterated in the Koran. Possibly, Islam provided the necessary unifying ideology to subdue and synthesize patriarchal tribes of Arabia, as well as other patriarchal tribes with different traditions.
4. Shekel was the old silver coin used by the Hebrews, ancient Babylonians and Phoenicians etc., as currency (cash) and also as a measure of weight.
5. 'Family honour' in this context means to secure the ethnic or racial purity of the family or lineage and to ensure that their offspring have not been tampered with by an outsider. Accordingly, 'women's modesty' is ensured by severe restrictions on their behaviour, dress and social interaction.
6. Veiling of women, as well as seclusion, were both pre-Islamic customs, applied for the sake of women's 'modesty'. They were only practised by the nobility or aristocracy of the Persian Empire in the 1st Century A.D. [Beck and Keddie, 1978].
7. In Islam and probably in other patriarchal religions, the ideal qualities expected of a normal, decent woman can be defined as: loyalty, obedience, shyness, delicacy and gentleness.
8. As evidence of witch-hunts show, up to the 18-19th Century, even in Europe women's sexuality was seen as 'active'.
9. In this sense *Fitna* means a beautiful, sexually irresistible woman. Women are regarded as the source of all men's difficulties and, especially in Islam, they were seen as purely erotic creatures.

10. *Qoys* is the immediate or nuclear family in Somali structure and its reference is always from the male line; children are patronymically linked to the clan-family (father agnatic generation).
11. *Purdah* means to veil or confine and seclude women and thus segregate the sexes and create the two worlds, one of men and one of women. The exigencies of the nomadic way of life prevented the application of purdah to Somali women.
12. For Somalis, as in any other Muslim society, especially in the Middle East, the concept of dignity (*sharaf*) and personal family honour (*karama*) seem mainly to concern the sexual comportment of the women, who can damage the family's *sharaf* and *karama* through loss of their own reputation and sexual decency. Therefore, family honour is safe as long as the unmarried girls of the family keep their virginity intact and follow the prescribed code of conduct.
13. *Dia* comes from the Arabic word *Diya*, (blood wit) which in Somali is called *mag*. *Dia* paying-group, in tribal law means, the blood money paid for a murder or other damages committed by any member of the tribal group.

3. Historical Perspectives

Genital mutilation of women in its various forms has been practised for the past two and a half thousand years in many different parts of the world. Its widespread prevalence has led to much discussion, and there are basically two main theories regarding its origins. One is that it began in the Middle East and was diffused from there to Africa. The other is that it developed independently in different societies at various periods in history. Due to the diversity of regions in which the practice has been found, there have been many superstitious as well as scientific explanations attached to its development. A common theme in almost all societies, despite cultural and religious diversity, is that of the inhibition of women's sexual desires. In Africa, the purpose of removing women's genital organs is to decrease their sexual appetite. We found that cases of clitoridectomy performed in Europe and the United States in the late 19th and early 20th Centuries were also justified on similar grounds.

In many societies, as we have said, guaranteed virginity of the bride has an economic significance; women are sewn up to be preserved for their future husband's pleasure and to prevent the possibility of an illegitimate child being conceived and born. In all of these societies, men's subjugation and control of women has been mystified by the promotion of such social values as: the honour of the family and husband, the initiation of girls into 'womanhood' (though genital mutilation destroys part of her 'womanhood'), the prevention of female sexual hysteria, etc. All of these conceal the real reasons responsible for the origin of the practice, which will be elaborated later in this chapter.

However, although there has been considerable mystification regarding the justification of the practice, it is also important to realize that over time it was not only the perceived (by men) necessity to subjugate women that has perpetuated the practice. Mystification itself has also played a primary role in its continuation.

While attempting to examine the historical background of the circumcision of women, the following questions will be raised: 1) Where did the custom originate? 2) Which class of women did it affect at the beginning? 3) Why was it initiated and how was it propagated?

To examine the past requires reliable, primary historical and documentary data, but written sources on the genital mutilation of women are rare, since this is an aspect of sexual practice, a subject involving a great deal of secrecy and taboo.

Details of the practice and the reasons given for it vary widely. Thus, such a custom which has diverse and controversial theories of origin would require extensive research quite beyond the scope of this study. My aim here is to provide a record of the incidence of female circumcision from such sources as are available, most of which consist of observations by travellers in the East, the Horn of Africa, Egypt and Sudan. No conclusive evidence exists to indicate where and when the custom started and how it spread. One common fact that all writers and researchers agree upon is that the circumcision of men (with a different purpose and quite different physical results) preceded the practice of circumcising women.

Probable Origins of Female Circumcision in Africa

The Ancient Egyptians

Male circumcision operations are represented in a relief on the tomb of Ankh-Ma-Hor of the 6th Dynasty (2340-2180 BC) [Baashir, 1977:1]. Other representations of Ancient Egypt also show circumcised penises, thus confirming that male circumcision has been practised in Egypt for many thousands of years; it is believed that male circumcision was known earlier among the Semitic peoples. It was adopted by the Israelites and later by the Phoenicians. Semitic tribes such as the Israelites lived in Egyptian slavery for a long time and may have adopted the custom from them.

Similar records for the circumcision of women do not exist, though many writers and travellers are of the opinion that it started in the same area as a parallel to the male operation. However, there is ample evidence that the custom of clitoridectomy and infibulation was practised among the Ancient Egyptians. According to many researchers, the oldest known source work that records the custom is that of Strabo, the Greek geographer and historian, c.25 BC, who visited Upper Egypt. He said: 'One of the customs most zealously observed among the Egyptians is this, that they rear every child that is born and *circumcise* the boys and excise the girls, as is also customary among the Jews, who are also Egyptians in origin.' [Meinardus, 1967:390]. What is interesting here is that Strabo differentiates between circumcision and excision. However, most modern writers on the subject seem to accept the explanation of Ghalioungui. Applied to both males and females, Ghalioungui explained the custom as follows:

> Although generally practised, this custom, which was probably an inheritance from ancestral puberty rites, was not so compulsory with the Egyptians as it was with the *Hebrew*, except in the sacerdotal and royal classes. Indeed, there are numerous drawings of uncircumcised persons. According to Strabo, girls were also subjected to it. But although the state of preservation of mummies does not allow any conclusion in that respect, the extension of the custom to girls must have occurred late, at least after the Exodus. Strabo must not, however, be believed too literally, because he says elsewhere and on two different occasions (XVIII, 5 and XVI, 37) that the Jews had taken the double custom from the Egyptians, which is obviously wrong since the Jews, who circumcise their males, never excised their females. [Ghalioungui, 1963:96].

On the other hand Meinardus [1967:389], quoting from a German text by Ernst Klippel points out that:

> Among the numerous and various eschatological expectations of the Ancient Egyptians, we find an interesting magical formula for the reviving of the dead. This formula includes among other things that he who wants to have understanding of this magic, must, first of all, recite the magical text, after having smeared his body with the . . . of an uncircumcised virgin and with the . . . of an uncircumcised old man.

The reference to the 'uncircumcised virgin', surely indicates that female circumcision was practised among the Ancient Egyptians, though many other examples indicate that it was not a general rule pertaining to all Egyptian men and women.

The reference also points at the link between female sexuality and magic. Magic in ancient times was seen as control over other natural forces, particularly fertility of earth, humans and animals to enhance productive forces generally. [Frazer, 1923:7]. In Ancient Egypt, women were seen as the *only* possessors of magic. When men wanted to obtain control over women's magic powers they imitated women, i.e., they wore women's clothes. The sexual mutilation of women might also be partly explained as an attempt to obtain control of this magic power which was perceived as being linked to women's independent sexuality.

According to Dr. Taba. famous historians such as Herodotus tell us that in the 5th Century BC female circumcision was practised by the Phoenicians, Hittites and Ethiopians as well as the Egyptians. In 1767, the German traveller Niebuhr, who was the sole survivor of the first European scientific expedition to Arabia, Egypt and Syria, reported the custom to be fairly prevalent in some countries of the Middle and Near East. [Taba, 1979:8].

Remondino, [Remondino, 1891] states that several other, older sources report female circumcision in Egypt, e.g. the London papyrus published by Peyron, the report of Bishop St. Ambrosius of Milan in 374 AD, and that of Aetios of Amido (Book 16) and Paulus Alginetes (Book 6) quoted in the original Greek by Sudhof (III:178. Note 3).

The Greek papyrus of the year 163 BC makes reference to an Egyptian woman living in Serapeum at Memphis and states that:

> The mother of Tothemis . . . came to him and represented that her daughter has reached the age for marriage and has to be circumcised according to the custom of the Egyptians. For this occasion the girl was considered as entering the period of womanhood and had to be provided with better clothing as well as dowry. [Meinardus, 1967:390].

In this connection it is clear that circumcision was an essential pre-marital rite for women in Egypt.

The practice among the Egyptians was also known to the moralists and physicians of the Roman world. St. Ambrosius wrote:

> The Egyptians circumcise their males at their fourteenth year, and the women are said to be circumcised in the same year, because from that very time the passion of sex begins

> to burn and the monthly period of the women begin. [Remondino, 1891:271; Meinardus, 1967:390].

As quoted by Meinardus, Karim and Roshdi, and Hosken, two Greek physicians (Aetius Amide, 6th Century AD; and Soramus, 138 AD) provided a detailed clinical description of the operation of female excision among the Egyptians, including the instruments that were used.

Both physicians claimed that the clitoris grows to a shameful size. Thus, Soramus is quoted as writing: 'In some cases the clitoris is so large that it presents a shameful deformity, so that when irritated by contact of garments it rises up and the woman is excited to venery.' He claimed to have treated such cases by clitoridectomy. He mentioned that only two instruments were used: a sharp scalpel and the myzon (ring-slide forceps with spoon-shaped, toothed jaws). He describes the operation thus: 'Lying the patient on her back with the feet together, with the myzon grip what is outside and seems to be too much . . . cutting it away with the scalpel and then healing the wound with the necessary care.' [Karim and Ammar, 1965:2].

Aetius quoted with approval the Egyptian custom of amputation of the clitoris:

> And in addition, with certain of the women their clitoris increases in growth and becomes unseemly and shameful, but also being continually rubbed by their clothes it excites them and rouses the desire for copulation; wherefore, on account of its increased size, the Egyptians determined to take it off, especially at the time when girls were ready to be married.

Aetius gave more precise surgical directions than Soramus for clitoridectomy at that time:

> They cause the girl to be seated on a stool, and a strong *young man* standing behind her, places his forearms beneath her thighs and buttocks so as to have control of her legs and her whole body. The operator standing in front of the girl seizes her clitoris with large forceps, pulling it out with his left hand, whilst with the right hand he cuts it off with the teeth of the forceps. It is necessary to make well the amount we intend to remove, so as not to take the clitoris away by

its roots, but only remove the superfluous part.

Aetius' description is interesting as the operation is performed by *men*, contrary to the present system; also the whole clitoris is not removed, at least among certain groups. This shows: 1) men, even then, were interested in controlling the clitoris, and 2) To remove the *whole* clitoris would perhaps have resulted in total frigidity, which men did not want.

Karim and Ammar mention another Greek physician, Paul Aegina (925–960 AD) who described the same operation, and stated that an enlarged clitoris is a problem. It is a shameful thing which could 'erect like a penis and make for lesbian coitus'. [Karim and Ammar, 1965:4].

Whether or not clitoridectomy existed at the same time elsewhere than is indicated in these quoted records is unknown; no other written records are available. Neither is there any clear indication which class of women was affected first. According to Strabo, inspection of royal female mummies, led some authorities to conclude that excision was first used by *high caste women of Egypt.* Modawi claims that a large number of circumcised mummies have been discovered, and thus surmises that excision was a feature of women's life among the *royalty* and privileged groups, but since the commoners and less privileged were not mummified it is not possible to ascterain how far this applied to women generally.

Some other sources also relate that a clitoridectomy was a sign of social distinction. According to Shandall, in Ancient Egypt, the practice was restricted to rulers and priestesses and their families. He points out that women from these social and economic spheres may have been unable to inherit property unless they had first undergone clitoridectomy. [Shandall, 1967:178]. Mary Daly, quoting Benoite Groult [Daly, 1975], claims that the mummies of both Cleopatra and Nefertiti have no clitoris.

In the early 19th Century, travellers from Egypt, as quoted by Widstrand relate that excision — but not infibulation — was practised on all Egyptian girls. 'However, infibulation was quite general in the case of female slaves to prevent them from becoming pregnant.' [Widstrand, 1965:95-124]. Meaning, to prevent them from intercourse, which obviously indicates that slave girls were used only for labour.

In this historical context, one might tentatively speculate upon the connection between excision of privileged (royalty, priestesses) women and the establishment of private property. Perhaps there should be clearer differentiation between clitoridectomy — as a measure to control female sexuality (magic), and infibulation, 'locking up a woman' and making her the property of one man. It seems reasonable to surmise that excision of the clitoris was the older form of the custom practised among the priestly caste and royalty, perhaps to establish the superiority of male magic (word-magic) over female (fertility) magic, and we might even venture to suggest this practice was simultaneous with the transition from the female moon-principle to the male sun-principle in Egypt.

Evidence thus exists that points to rites of passage involving genital mutilation first of royal and aristocratic women. It is reasonable to suppose that it spread from royalty to the rest of society (with more severe modification for slaves) as well as diffusing geographically.

According to Hosken [1978:12], Widstrand also reported that infibulated slave girls were brought to Egypt mostly from the south, from Nubia and the Sudan, and 'the slave dealers took care to acquire infibulated girls, who naturally fetched a higher price on the Egyptian markets'.

Other sources relate that the slave markets in East Africa were mainly for female slaves, especially young girls brought by Arab traders; the mortality rate among women was very high due to poverty and hunger that mainly affected women as they faced social discrimination and exploitation in their families and societies.

Circumcision of Women in Somalia and Other Red Sea Areas

Rituals in connection with virginity, circumcision, marriage, and childbirth which are dominant in the Middle East are prevalent in much of Africa, especially among the Red Sea tribes and in sub-Sahara Africa. In these parts, a boy may not marry unless he is circumcised; the same applies to excision which has acquired much the same rhetoric and similar justifications.

The position of women both in Red Sea and Arab African (Middle Eastern) societies is similar, and for similar reasons to that I have described in Chapter 2 women and girls are the property of men; girls are regarded as an economic asset bringing wealth and alliance into the family and clan by marriage etc. etc. Strict seclusion of women, however, is impossible among some ethnic groups, such as the nomadic women in Somalia, Sudan, Eritrea,

Oromos and women in subsistence farming in Egyptian Nubia as well as the sub-Saharan African women in such countries as Mali and Senegal. Hence, infibulation was the most effective means to keep the girls' virginity intact, and thus to ensure the highest bride-price.

Since there is some historical evidence to show that Egypt and the Nile Valley was a centre for genital operations, one may wonder if this custom was taken from the Egyptians, or was spread to these areas by the Arab conquerors and traders. It is my opinion that it may have come from Egypt, through Arab conquerors who probably had an economic interest to establish a monopoly over all women as potential slaves, or wives, or to be exchanged for wealth (bride-price). To do that they may have used the 'technology' found in Egypt.

A Venetian historian, Petro Bembo, secretary to Pope Leo X, in a posthumous history published in the middle of the 16th Century, on the basis of the accounts of travellers to the Red Sea stated: 'These areas are inhabited by black, excellent men, brave in War.' Bembo describes that in this part of Africa, virginity is held in such high esteem that: 'The private parts of girls are sewn together immediately after birth . . . when adult the girls are given away in marriage . . . The husband's first measure is to cut open with a knife the solidly consolidated private parts of the virgin.' [Widstrand, 1964:102]. Hosken also reported that Widstrand, in his research into infibulation, mentions Strabo, who described the population living along the east coast of the Red Sea, which he called: 'mutilated people'. Strabo stated that they: 'excise' their women like the Egyptians, while he describes others as 'circumcised'. [Hosken, 1979:10].

Other information comes from Major J.S. King, who had spent some time in the East and the Horn of Africa. He describes the operation in much the same way as in earlier chapters here. After the wedding ceremony (the bride was about 15 years old): 'Some young men take a pride in piercing what may be called the velum virginale with no other instrument than that furnished by nature, but in general a knife is used.' The operation is usually performed by an experienced woman, and, 'The husband holds the wife to prevent her from struggling.' Despite all the complications resulting from the operation, the 'Somalis themselves admit that infibulation is a relic of paganism, but they are so thoroughly conservative, in the worst sense of the word, that they dare not relinquish the custom.' [King, 1890:2-6].

According to Melly, who also studied the Somali:

> Whether the removal of the nymphae and clitoris is intended further to reduce the risk of premarital intercourse by diminshing sensation, or whether these amputations are employed with the sole object of obtaining raw surfaces for suture and closure, remain a matter for conjecture. Native opinion takes the attitude that this is the customary procedure, and it has apparently been unquestioningly adopted from one generation to another. . . . It seems likely, however, that the details of the whole operation were in the beginning deliberately planned to ensure virginity both by lessening desire and by creating a definite physical obstruction to its fulfilment. The originators may have had an even longer vision and in incorporating the amputations perhaps had in view the discouragement of unfaithfulness in the future wives of the race — a sort of Somali chastity belt. [Melly, 1935: 1272].

Despite the scanty nature of written material regarding the origin of the practice of infibulation among Somali and other Red Sea tribes, there is sufficient evidence to suggest that, due to the strong cultural ties that existed for centuries between the Red Sea coastal tribes and Ancient Egypt, possibly the practice of infibulation was diffused from Pharaonic Egypt to Somalia and the other coastal areas. The exact origin of this custom, whether in Somalia, Egypt or other African societies, however, cannot be established with any degree of confidence.

It might be worthwhile to summarize the political economic significance of the custom here as it appears to me.

1. Excision began in Ancient Egypt as a measure to control female sexuality and magic in the transition from early agriculture to systematic cultivation of the Nile Valley; it was not yet a property relation.

2. Second phase. from nomadism to trade: (a) Trade in slaves, also slave girls, went along with Arab conquest. This was a mode of production to accumulate wealth not produced by that society. It needed superior weapons for wars and feuds over camels, cattle, land or slave girls. Women became property (like cattle or land). Violent acquisition of women as exchangeable property for trade became a mode of acquiring wealth. Virginity became a 'trade mark'. (b) Regular trade of women in the marriage market.

Virginity as economic value-related to male property rights over cattle, camels, land and other wealth.

The Practice in Other Parts of the World

For various reasons, female circumcision has been practised in many parts of the world, while the practice has still remained commoner in Africa than elsewhere. Many researchers indicate that no continent in the world has not, at some time, engaged in the practice. [Sequeira, 1931:1054; Worsley, 1938:688; Hathout, 1963:505; Taba, 1979:8; Baashir, 1977:2].

Asia

Many travellers and researchers confirmed that the circumcision of women was prevalent among peoples of the Arabian peninsula long before Islam. Sir Richard Francis Burton (1821–90), the great traveller, described his experiences in his books about Asia, Africa and the Americas. He reported, in a footnote (in Latin) in the book on his pilgrimage to Mecca and Medina, that circumcision among the Arabs is the practice for both sexes, and he related the story of Prophet Ibrahim. Excision, the amputation of the clitoris (the seat of pleasure, according to Aristotle) is performed, as otherwise, he was told, the women would be insatiable and indulge excessively in sexual intercourse. [Hosken, 1979:9].

Both Sequeira and Worsley mention a similar practice and rationale in Asia among such ethnic groups as Kamatchkans; Malays of the East Indian Archipelago; Alfurese Archipelago (most islands). [Sequeira, 1931:1054; Worsley, 1938:689].

Australia and Latin America

Worsley mentions that the Pitta-Patta aborigines of Australia practised the most drastic form of female mutilation called introcision, which he describes as follows:

> When the girl reaches puberty, the whole tribe, both sexes, assembled. The operator, an elderly man trained for the purpose, enlarges the vaginal orifice by tearing it downwards with three fingers bound round with opossum string . . . In other districts the perineum is split up with a stone knife. This is usually followed by compulsory sexual intercourse with a number of young men, and even yet more disquieting

practices, for the rejuvenation of the tribal aged and infirm. [Worsley, 1938:688].

Worsley, Sequeira and Remondino reported that the practice has also been traced in Eastern Mexico, Peru and Brazil. Remondino, quoting Alfred Reich and Felix Stegelmann, mentions that among the Conibos, a division of the Pano Indians in north eastern Peru, circumcision and opening of the vagina are performed. For Indians in Peru, Remondino quoted the following passage from Winterstein:

> As soon as a girl has attained maturity, a feast is arranged, in which mashato, an intoxicating drink brewed from manioc roots, plays a large part. The girl is made insensibly drunk and then subjected to the operation. An old woman, in the presence of the roaring tribe, performs it with a bamboo knife while the girl lies stretched out on three posts. She cuts around the hymen from the *introitus vaginae*, severs the hymen from the labia, at the same time exposing the clitoris. Then she paints the bleeding parts with medical herbs and after a while introduces into the vagina a slightly moistened penis made from clay which conforms exactly in size and shape to that of her betrothed. [Remondino, 1891:273].

According to Remondino (p.274) the men of this group were not circumcised.

The objectives of genital operations on women among the tribes mentioned in Australia and South America are different from the African/Arabian ones. It seems from the descriptions that the vagina is forcibly opened to ensure — in a young, perhaps unwilling girl — easier penetration for the penis. In most cases the clitoris is not removed, nor are the women sewn up to ensure virginity, but the intention to secure domination of women's sexuality by men through violence is clear.

Europe and the United States of America

In the continent of Europe, the practice was confined to the Russian Skoplozy, a Christian sect. The Skoplozy also practised the ritual in order to ensure perpetual virginity. Worsley points out that the Skoplozy perform the operation with exceptional severity, ablating even the upper parts of the labia majora, quoting Saint Matthew (XIX-12) as their authority: 'There be eunuchs that have made themselves eunuchs for the kingdoms of the heaven's sake.' [Worsley, 1938:689; Sequeira, 1931:1054].

In 19th Century Europe, and later in the United States some doctors developed a thesis that the excision of the female clitoris cures various psycho-sexual problems, such as insanity, epilepsy and hysteria. In 1866, a French writer, Richeraud, reported the case of a young woman who was addicted to masturbation and, when her parents took her to Professor Dubois, he cured her by removing the clitoris with one stroke of the bistoury, and prevented the bleeding with an application of the cautery. [Karim and Ammar, 1965:4].

In 1858, Dr. Isaac Baker Brown, an English gynaecologist first performed clitoridectomy on women to check mental disorders. In 1866 he published his remarks on the operation of clitoridectomy, which he had performed on many women. Brown's thesis was that nervous affectation complicating diseases of the female genitalia were the direct result of 'peripheral excitement of the pudic nerve', (i.e., masturbation). Brown was strongly opposed on that point and was censured by his professional society. He died in 1873 and the performance of clitoridectomy in Europe died with him. [Fleming, 1960:1018].

Barker Benfield relates that clitoridectomy was practised in the United States (following its introduction in England in the late 1860s) until almost 1925. He reports that clitoridectomy was superseded by the circumcision of girls and women of all ages up to menopause; a practice that continued until 1937. It was said that the purpose of both processes in the United States was to check the incidence of female masturbation, an activity which men feared and thought was growing, and which inevitably aroused women's naturally boundless but often oppressed sexual desires. [Benfield, 1976].

Another widespread practice, observed mostly in the United States in the late 19th Century, flourishing between 1880 and 1900 and only decreasing in the first decade of the 20th Century, was the operation of 'normal ovariotomy'. In addition to that, other means of negating intrinsically feminine functions were largely replaced by operations such as hysterectomy,[1] mastectomy,[2] etc. Barker Benfield points out, 'In North America a woman was supposed to be dependent, submissive, unquenchably supportive, smiling, imparting an irrelevant morality, regarding sex as something to be endured and her own organs as somehow a dirty if necessary disease.' [1976:122].

These attitudes were imposed by men and further resulted in the development of the idea that due to the menstrual and reproductive functions of women, they were particularly liable to mental illness and criminal activity. Gardner specifically described menstruation as an infirmity and that as 'it was a crime to be sick', women were criminals by nature. [Benfield, 1976:123].

In 19th Century US, women's sexuality was generally seen as something repulsive, dirty and abnormal, while that of men was natural and healthy. Any attempt by women to break out of these stereotyped sex roles was interpreted by men as the desire to usurp men's place in society and consequently a threat for which female 'castration' was one cure. It was claimed that clitoridectomy not only reduced a women's unnatural sexuality but also elevated her moral sense. In the words of an 1893 proponent of such practices: 'The patient becomes tractable, orderly, industrious, and cleanly.' [Benfield:122].

Thus, the history of the sexual mutilation of women in any of its various manifestations must concern itself not only with where these were, as well as where they still are practised, but also consider the motives for these operations at various stages of history.

Some Reasons Advanced for the Practice

Over the years, various reasons have been given to explain the motives for circumcising women. In many cases the custom has been practised due to traditional myths and misleading interpretations, and under the pretext of adherence to health and to religious principles.

The opinion that the operation was for 'aesthetic reasons', as reported by the medical writers quoted in the previous section, especially their statements and descriptions of the 'notorious hypertrophy' of the labia minora and unusual enlargement of the clitoris is not supported by modern medical evidence, or even any first-hand observation as to the nature of this alleged hypertrophy. It was only considered to be a blemish and therefore efforts must be made to remove these organs; no scientific basis was offered for considering them a blemish.

Of the many other mythological reasons which attempt to explain the importance of female circumcision, some of the most common ones are: as a religious sacrifice; for hygienic reasons;

as an initiation rite; as a means of attenuating sexual desire and rendering the woman less vulnerable to sexual temptation; to safeguard virginity and act to ensure virginity until marriage; upholding the tradition of the Prophet, etc.

Many views and descriptions have been advanced to explain these reasons. While referring to Holy Writ, Sequeira [1931:1055] indicated that circumcision was viewed in old Egypt as:

> . . . it has been surmised that the operation was introduced as a sanitary measure, but its great antiquity and its practice in some of the races mentioned seems to negate this view. Moreover, this reason would not apply in the case of the female. There seems to be no doubt that the rite was first performed on the male. There is considerable evidence in favour of a religious significance, and that a sacrifice was made of part of the body for the salvation of the whole. Some references in the Holy Writ indicate that it was an outward and visible sign of an inward and spiritual grace (e.g. 'circumcision of the heart', Deuteronomy XXX, v.30, Romans ii, v.29 and C). Some authorities look upon the operation as a sacrifice to the deity presiding over fertility, but it is questionable if it was introduced to increase sexual gratification.

Sequeira's explanation is idealistic and his attitude is perhaps typical of Roman Catholicism in its spiritualization of pain for the 'sake of God'.

Other references report that Pharaonic circumcision goes back to the Ancient Egyptians when temples existed for virgins, and when virgins were sacrificed to the Gods. The Pharaonic operation was to ensure their virginity. [Ismail, 1977].

In relation to initiation rites into the tribe, Sequeira gives another explanation:

> There is no doubt that in both sexes circumcision was and is looked upon as an initiation into the tribe. As a rule an uncircumcised girl cannot enter society. Mohammedans who observe the rite do not permit women to enter the mosque until after its performance. In Ancient Egypt, girls could not marry or inherit property before submitting to the operation. As already indicated, its non-performance is still held by certain tribes to render a woman unfit for

> marriage. It is said to be a direct insult to apply the term 'uncircumcised' to an Abyssinian woman, and in Old Calabar it is grounds for divorce. Fortitude during the ceremony is greatly esteemed by the relatives and others present, but it seems hardly likely that such an ordeal was devised as a test of endurance as some have suggested. [Sequeira, 1931:1055].

Many societies in Africa who practice female circumcision looked upon it as a mark of distinction or an initiation into womanhood, but Herbert Spencer and many others claim that it was a mark of subjugation. [Shandall, 1967:178]. The same conception is expressed in Ghalioungui, [1973:93], who writes that:

> Every person was believed to have both male and female souls, each located in different parts of the genitalia. Possibly as a result of some sort of comparative anatomy that supposes, however, an unexpected anatomical insight, or merely as a coincidence, the male soul in girls was located in the vestigial phallus, i.e. the clitoridial eminence; and the female soul in boys was placed in the prepuce, taken to represent the labia. According to that view, young individual adolescents had to shed their heterosexual outfit before qualifying as integral members of their sex community.

Ghalioungui's explanation is physiologically correct. In West Africa a similar belief is reported by Hosken when she quotes Diallo's research on excision among the Bambara, the largest population group in Mali:

> It is believed, traditionally, that the clitoris in the female and the prepuce of the male are the seat of an evil force called 'Wanzo'. This Wanzo prevents a girl or a boy from having intercourse with the opposite sex, and it also prevents its owner from entering the world of the adults. Therefore, the double necessity of removing this impediment and affirming the sex of each person. Naturally, such an operation is not without risk; hence, the need for all kinds of ritual. The child, as long as it retains its 'Wanzo' is considered polluted, because it is both male and female. The Wanzo is responsible for preventing people from knowing themselves and from knowing God. Therefore, boys who are not circumcised and girls who are not excised, are not allowed to speak to adults,

> and are considered ignorant among the Bambara. These are beliefs which go back to ancient times. Only recently, some outside influences are changing the practices.

This Bambara explanation given by Diallo seems plausible, but in respect of Egyptian Nubia Kennedy declares that '. . . no role of transition or passage in the sense usually assumed by analysts of such rituals' can be connected with a clitoridectomy. In Kennedy's opinion both male and female circumcision is a *rite of passage* but not one which is associated with the transition from childhood to adulthood but with the much more important transition from low status of bachelorhood to the full status of marriage.

Kennedy states that: 'The Nubians argue that the only way to blunt the sexual wildness of girls and preserve their chastity is through the means of clitoridectomy and infibulation — expressing the belief that women have an inherently wanton character which is physiologically centred in the clitoris.' [Kennedy, 1970:181].

Sierra Leonian girls after excision are given a new name and kept in absolute seclusion until their hand is asked in marriage. [Shandall, 1967:179].

The reason given for the practice by one Sudanese man is very interesting:

> Circumcision of women releases them from their bondage to sex, and enables them to fulfil their real destiny as mothers. The clitoris is the basis for female masturbation — such masturbation is common in a hot climate; the spiritual basis of masturbation is fantasy; in fantasy a woman broods on sexual images; such brooding inevitably leads a woman to spiritual infidelity, since she commits adultery in her heart, and this is the first step to physical infidelity, which is the breaker of homes. [Vern L. Bullough, 1976:143].

Many of the sources quoted mentioned that infibulation is customary among people where girls often have to be together with men; in some other societies, such as in south east Africa, women are believed to be protected by living in seclusion. Shandall reports that infibulation was practised by ancient Arabs, long before Islam, to protect the shepherd girls against male attacks while they were grazing their sheep. [Shandall, 1967:179].

In the same connection, Remondino, whose book is a collection of facts and stories from many parts of the world, relates that:

> Infibulation was known . . . for centuries and in those days [and] rude times it seemed as the most natural and effective mode of accomplishing the object (to ensure chastity). It was not as barbarous an operation as emasculation of the male, as it only temporarily interfered with [the woman's] functions.
> In the old world the practice is still performed in various manners. In Ethiopia, when a female child is born, the vulva is stitched together, allowing only the necessary passage for the needs of nature. These parts adhere together and the father is then possessed of a virgin which he can sell to the highest bidder, the union being severed with a sharp knife just before marriage. In some parts of Africa and Asia a ring transfixed the labia, which to be removed, required either a file or a chisel; this is worn only by virgins. Married women wear a sort of mussle fastened around the body, locked by means of a key and padlock, the key being only in the possession of the husband. The wealthy have their seraglios and eunuchs that take the place of the belt and the lock. Another method is a belt worn about the hips, made of brass wire, with a secret combination of fastenings, known only to the husband. In the museum in Naples are to be seen some of the belts, studded with sharp pointed spikes over the abdominal part of the instrument, which was calculated to prevent even innocent familiarity . . . to say nothing of greater evils. [Remondino, 1891:51].

Remondino also mentioned that in the past, rape was punished by cutting off the male's genitalia, and this punishment formed part of the penal code of the Egyptians. The same punishment was also used by the Spaniards and British. But rape he writes: '. . . being one of the most complex and intricate of medico-legal subjects, by the difficulty of proving the crime, as well as the ease with which the crime could be charged through motives of revenge, spite or cupidity . . . resulted evidently in the punishment going out of use'. [Remondino, 1891:97].

As a corollary, it seems that women were made to pay the price for rape in advance, by being mutilated, infibulated and segregated, while in Middle Eastern and African societies men are encouraged to prove their virility. The promotion of men's sexual freedom seemingly led to women's infibulation in order to convert them into sexually insensible machines for the greater security of the husband as his private property.

Shandall, quoting Schaefer, [1955] has given an historically interesting description of the means of guaranteeing chastity in Oriental women. He described that a bamboo stick, eight inches long, was inserted into the vagina, strapped with a shield and locked, during the absence of their husbands; the key was in the keeping of a eunuch. [Shandall, 1967:179].

Another device, reported by many historians, to maintain women's chastity was employed by mediaeval knights who, when travelling, would take the key to their wife's chastity belt to prevent them committing adultery in their absence.

Throughout the 19th Century, the importance of virginity in brides was stated to be the reason for infibulation, both to safeguard virginity and to ensure pre-marital chastity.

Widstrand states: 'Infibulation, as distinct from excision, is practised mainly in the Middle East, due to the importance attached to virginity by Muslims.' This certainly contradicts the view that Islam is tolerant of female sexual pleasure and it is an ignorance of the teachings of the Prophet that the clitoris is the source of all sexual passion in women and not to be destroyed.

Religion as a Justification

The role of world religions in the spread of the practice of female circumcision also seems to be controversial. While practised mainly in Muslim countries today, it did not originate with the rise of the Islamic religion; evidence for this is the common claim that it existed among some pre-Islamic peoples of the Arabian Peninsula. Barclay [1964:158] and Seligman [1913:639-646] believe that it was practised in Sudan prior to the introduction of Islam.

Although always entangled in beliefs and superstitions with a mystical or religious background, the various peoples who practice female circumcision do not conform to any common racial, social or religious pattern, as can be seen from the global distribution of the practice. Despite the fact that all the literature stressed that genital mutilation is not a religious rite, but rather that it is a custom of the people or certain ethnic groups, religious authorities have rarely opposed the custom formally. Muslims, Christians and other religious groups in Africa, circumcise their daughters. In those animistic societies where the practice existed it was clearly connected with ancestor worship, as was attested by statements that it was done because it is 'the wish of the ancestors'.

The origin of women's excision among the Copts is linked to a legend about Abraham and his two co-wives Sarah (Sara) and Hagar (Agar). Meinardus [1967:391] relates the legend by Michael, the 12th Century Coptic Orthodox Metropolitan of Damielta, who explains that the custom spread among the Christians of Egypt on account of the 'Victory of the Circumcised', i.e. the Jews. The story confirms that female circumcision came into being during the time of Abraham. The legend is as follows:

> Abraham was married to his cousin Sarah and they lived together for many years without having any children. In the end Abraham married a slave girl called Hagar (another version is that Hagar was Sarah's Egyptian servant). Sarah and Hagar became co-wives and Abraham had a son with Hagar, called Ismail, and another with Sarah, called Isahaq. After some time, the relationship between the co-wives Sarah and Hagar deteriorated. Sarah ill-treated Hagar and one day excised Hagar and sent her out of the house. According to this story, female circumcision occurred because of Sarah's jealousy. Hagar, after that, took her son Ismail and went to Hijaz. Her son Ismail grew up to be very handsome and God beautified him in the eyes of the women and they asked his mother to give him in marriage. At that time Hagar said: 'We are circumcised people, both male and female and we do not marry except with those like us.' Then, when the women had circumcised themselves, Ismail married them, and God fulfilled his promise to him, and granted to him twelve princesses. Circumcision then spread in that country and in the countries which were neighbouring to it. It became firmly established among the Copts of Egypt when they witnessed the Victory of God for the circumcised, namely the Children of Israel. [Meinardus, 1967:391].

Whether or not this legend is based on fact, it is true that oriental Jewesses were circumcised. [Remondino, 1891:271]. It seems that religious traditions, interpreted by men to maintain a subordinate role for women, will continue — whatever its damaging effects — until it is challenged by women. An interesting example is concerned with Roman Catholic missionaries in Ethiopia.

Sequeira [1931:1054] states that the Roman Catholic missionaries who came to Abyssinia in the 16th Century, wanted to forbid female circumcision among their converts. The result was that no Abyssinian would marry a Catholic girl unless she was circumcised. 'Then the Catholic community diminished and the people returned to their heathen misconceptions.' The problem was reported to Rome from where a surgeon, Paulus Aiginetes was sent to investigate if the operation was necessary in Ethiopia; he formally declared that it was essential, on the basis that a congenital hypertrophy of the pudenda is common among Abyssinian women. The missionaries therefore permitted the practice to continue.

All the major religions are male centred and this infers the ready acceptance of any means to curb the traditionally asserted recalcitrance of women and to ensure that they are sexually 'correct' according to the moral tenets and concepts of sexual purity adduced from their religions. Even if they do not traditionally circumcise women, the evilness of sex and the dangers of women were carried over into the mainstream of Western thought and Western medical science, at least until the mid-20th Century.

Though the Koran is silent on the subject of female circumcision, and cannot be regarded by practising Muslims as a command of God, Islamic jurists, however, interpreted that often quoted Hadith of Om Attiya and others as favouring female circumcision. It is reported that the Prophet Mohamed told a woman in Medina who performed female circumcision: 'Touch but do not destroy. It is more illuminating to the woman and more enjoyable to the husband.' Another version of this statement of the Prophet says: 'Do not go deep. This is enjoyable to the woman and is preferable to the husband.'

In these statements, the Prophet advised minimizing excision (simply removing the prepuce rather than total clitoridectomy), and other extensive operations such as are practised in Somalia and Sudan.

Hamed Ammer quotes another Hadith which is attributed to the Prophet and which states: 'Circumcision is my way for men, but is merely ennobling for women.' With respect to the teachings of the four Islamic Schools of Law in this subject, Sheikh Ibrahim Mahrous, Chairman of the Fatwa Committee in El Azhar in 1951 reported that according to Imam El Shafie, circumcision is regarded as a *duty* for both men and women.

The Melekites based their opinion on the Prophet's saying, which was handed down successively by many learned men, that circumcision was a tradition in men and an *embellishment* in women, while Hanifites and Hanbalites describe it as sunna (tradition) for men and *ennobling* for women.

According to Maria Assaad [1979:13], in 1951, eight eminent Muslim leaders interviewed by Lewa-a El Islam in Egypt, for the purpose of giving clarification on female circumcision all agreed that only the milder form (Type 1) is sunna for men and ennobling for women. To support this view the Grand Mufti of Egypt Fadilat in 1951 quoted the following *fatwa* registered on 11 September 1950 in Dar-El Ifta under number 280/63:

> Female circumcision is an Islamic practice mentioned in the tradition of the Prophet and sanctioned by Imams and Jurists, in spite of their differences on whether it is a duty or a sunna (tradition). We support the practice as *sunna* and sanction it in view of its effect on attenuating the sexual desire in women and directing it to the desirable moderation.

Some learned men have disputed Abu Hurair's Hadith in this connection as conveyed from the Prophet: 'Islam is the religion of purity and purity is accomplished by five deeds: circumcision, the removal of pubic hair, trimming of moustaches, paring of the nails and plucking of hair from under the armpits.'

Learned Muslim men have, however, disagreed as to the meaning of purity, the majority insisted that it is a tradition while others say that it has the force of religion. At the same time they are all agreed that these five things were not all obligatory (including circumcision).

In conclusion, it is clear that religious interpretations vary over time and place, and, as we can see, the later ones of modern Imams are more repressive of independent female sexuality. There is enough evidence to show that the attitude of Islam towards the sexual pleasure and enjoyment of both sexes is positive rather than the reverse. This is confirmed and emphasized by the Prophet, in for example, a statement such as: 'Touch but do not destroy. This is enjoyable to the woman and is preferable to the husband', and was obviously intended to counteract the prevailing social trend which was obviously intended to counteract the prevailing social trend which was in favour of reducing women's sexual pleasure. At the time of the Prophet, it seems it was considered necessary that both men and women should experience sexual pleasure and fulfilment.

Since few women can read all of the Islamic text, they are led to believe that their mutilation is a religious command. For example, Islamization is still progressing in West Africa, in such countries as Mali, Senegal, Upper Volta, Mauritania, etc., therefore, it was reported that the local religious men and chiefs reinforce genital operations by telling the people that the operations have religious importance and that they are demanded by the Koran. Indeed, one of the worst insults in Muslim Africa is to be called 'Son of an uncircumcised mother'.

Although almost all the eminent Muslim leaders emphasized the fact that female circumcision does not lie in the domain of strict religious injunction to be closely adhered to by all Muslims, at the same time the previous arguments, while indicating a dispute over interpretation of the Prophet's words, substantiate the view that female circumcision has been promoted by Islamic leaders.

It is the responsibility of women to challenge the multiplicity of interpretation of religions and legends that are deliberately employed to sanction practices which mutilate them physically and damage them psychologically.

Most striking, perhaps, about the history of circumcision of women are the changes in rationale, significance, social function and ideology according to the transitions undergone by the societies where it is practised. The various explanations and mystifications offered to justify the practice; the masculine attitudes revealed; and the ideologies that evolved to support and perpetuate female circumcision, all emanate from men's motive to control women economically and sexually and as personal objects. Also through the various religious doctrines and their moral and ethical value systems, beliefs and traditions, women were made to fear their own sexuality and see it as a disease and crime. The process of women's mutilation and sexual negation also derives from men's concern to keep women as their exclusive, private objects.

Notes

1. Hysterectomy (the surgical removal of the uterus, sometimes also the Fallopian tubes and the ovaries) and ovariotomy (the removal of one or both ovaries) were usually — as today — performed for good medical reasons; nevertheless, there is evidence that some were performed, often without the woman's knowledge or consent, for quite other reasons at the instigation of her husband or parents, or even on the initiative of a physician.
2. Mastectomy is surgical removal of the breast(s), a radical mastect-

omy includes removing the muscles and lymph glands. It is impossible to understand what purpose this would serve except in cases of malignant growths.

4. A Small Community Study

A limited pilot study of a sample of 110 people, 70 women and 40 men, was undertaken in an attempt to investigate community attitudes towards the custom of female circumcision in Somalia. Special emphasis was laid on the social and health complications arising from the custom, and its future prospects.

It must be made clear, however, that this was a preliminary study of limited scope and cannot be considered as representative but must be viewed within this limited context. Nevertheless, certain conclusions can be drawn from this exercise upon which a deeper study could be based in the future.

Methodology

This study was carried out in Mogadiscio, the capital of the Somali Democratic Republic, during four weeks of fieldwork in 1980. The main objectives were:
1) to explore and identify important psychological, physical and social aspects of the problem, which could also be used as a guide for future studies;
2) to examine the magnitude of the practice at present and its perpetuation in the future, with special emphasis on: why, how, where and by whom the operation is performed;
3) to discover the attitudes of women (the people directly affected) in connection with the continuation or abolition of the practice;
4) to also discover the views of men, since the practice is, to a large extent initiated by them and serves their interests.

Two questionnaires were used; one with 62 questions for women (as they are the main target group) and one with 23 questions for men (see Appendixes 1 and 2).

As some members of the sample were unable to read or write the following methods had to be used: 1) the questionnaire was filled individually by respondents who could read and write; 2) for those who were unable to read and write the questionnaire was administered by the writer; 3) group interview-guided conversation according to the specific nature of the questions, was used with groups of women who were unable to read and write.

I concentrated mainly on two areas for the selection of women respondents. One was an out-patients' gynaecology clinic where I was able to avail myself of the help of the medical staff in administering the interview. The second was Government Ministries and Agencies where there were more women able to read and write and who were less suspicious of the questions or of the research.

For men also, I concentrated on Government Ministries and Agencies where I interviewed staff members and also other male members of the public who came there for services.

Sample Selected

The sample consisted of 70 women, aged between 20-60 years; the 40 men were in a similar age range as shown in Table 1.

The respondents were born in various regions of the Somali territories and were of varying educational levels, occupational status, and with different socio-economic backgrounds.

Table 1
Age and Marital Status of Respondents

	Women					*Men*				
Age Group	*M*	*D*	*W*	*S*	*Total*	*M*	*D*	*W*	*S*	*Total*
20 - 40	34	9	—	10	*53*	12	3	1	8	*24*
41 - 60	9	3	5	—	*17*	12	1	3	—	*16*
Total:	*43*	*12*	*5*	*10*	*70*	*24*	*4*	*4*	*8*	*40*

Key: M = Married; D = Divorced; W = Widowed; S = Single.

Though both groups were ethnically Somalis, and Muslims by faith, the sample is not strictly random, due firstly to the time constraint; the period of about 20 days for interviews and distribution of questionnaires was inadequate for planning and selecting a random sample. Secondly, in this short period of time, access to a wider public, which is a necessary component of a random sample, was not possible.

The 62 questions scheduled for the women were divided into five main sections:

a) Background data of the respondent;
b) Sexual experience of the respondent with infibulated women;
c) Marital and sexual experiences;
d) The respondents perception of their spouse and the society's views on the practice of female circumcision;
e) Attitudes of the respondent to the practice and her understanding of the underlying physical and socio-economic implications.

The questionnaire for the men was divided into four main parts:

a) Background data of the respondent,
b) Sexual experience of the respondent with infibulated women,
c) The respondent's perception of the society's view on the practice of female circumcision,
d) The attitudes of the respondent towards the practice and his understanding of its implications.

Findings of the Survey

Background of the Respondents

Two thirds of the women interviewed were born in urban areas and one third in rural areas. Of the men 50% were born in urban, and 50% in rural areas.

As illustrated in Table 1, the study is concentrated mainly on two age groups — 20-40 and 41-60 years — among the women because they are important target groups for any future action against the practice, being already in the marriage and child-bearing stage which, to a large extent, will determine the fate of the women of the coming generation.

As we can see from this Table, the majority of the women in the age group 20 to 40, were married, in contrast with the situation of the men in the same age group of whom only 3 were married. This Table clearly indicates that women marry much earlier than men. A number of reasons for this can be suggested, for example: the qualities of an ideal wife are to be simple, naive and very young in age. Experience, knowledge of life and maturity are considered as something undesirable and even shameful for a woman. Men, on the other hand, usually marry later because of economic considerations, i.e., he has to provide a bride-price and a good standard of living for his future family, as he is regarded as the sole bread-winner.

Table 2 shows the distribution of ages at marriage of women respondents and the number of times they married. This Table illustrates the existence of a relatively high divorce rate and multiple marriages among 27% of the sample, and it is possible that there is a risk of divorce among the younger members of the sample.

The divorce rate within Somalia as a whole is high, though I am unable to find exact figures on the frequency of marriages and divorces. These are very common, especially among the lower socio-economic groups.

Table 2
Distribution of Women, according to Age at First Marriage/Number of Marriages

	Married			
Age Group	*Once*	*2–3 Times*	*4–5 Times*	*Total*
10–14	6	2	2	10
15–20	23	8	1	32
21–25	10	2	—	12
26–30	5	1	—	6
Total	*44*	*13*	*3*	*60*

Table 2 clearly shows that those women married at younger ages manifest a high incidence of divorces or multiple marriages. The data collected suggests that there could be a relationship between the ill-effects and complications of circumcision during marriage and childbirth and the high divorce rate. For example, 10 out of 16 women who had been married more than once reported that they left their first husbands because of this horrifying sexual experience which had resulted in their hatred and fear of their husbands.

Scope of the Practice

The study revealed that all the 70 women interviewed were circumcised. 57 women had had a Pharaonic circumcision or infibulation, 9 women had had a Sunna circumcision and 4 women had had a clitoridectomy.

Out of the total sample, 10 cases reported that infibulation was performed upon them more than once.[1] 19 had already had their daughters infibulated, while the daughters of a further 6 had already had the Sunna type operation; all respondents with sisters reported that they, and other female relatives above the age of 5, were circumcised.

Table 3
Age of Respondents at First Circumcision

Age	*Number of Girls*	*% of Total*
5	10	14%
6	15	21%
7	11	16%
8	10	14%
9	9	13%
10	8	11%
11	3	4%
12	2	3%
13	2	3%
Total	*70*	*99%*

From Table 3 we learn that the majority of women (55) were circumcised before the age of 10, which shows that the customary tendency is towards early circumcision.

Conditions Under Which Operations Are Performed
The study revealed that the majority (54) of the operations were performed by traditional midwives, while trends towards greater use of trained midwives were increasing among the younger age group of the urban middle class families; 16 operations were reportedly performed by trained midwives.

Regarding instruments used for the operations: those circumcised by traditional midwives reported that knives and razor blades were used for cutting, and thorns for joining the wound, whereas for operations performed by the trained midwives modern facilities like surgical scissors for cutting, catgut sutures for sewing, anaesthesia for relieving pain and antibiotics for preventing infections were employed.

I asked all the women what they felt when getting ready for the operation. They answered as follows: 57% (40 cases) — excited and frightened; 20% (14 cases) — mixed feelings of joy and worry; 16% (11 cases) — curious and eager to know what happens; 7% (5 cases) — could not remember their exact feelings.

Complications Arising
This study has shown that most of the women were circumcised in the Pharaonic way. This, as we have noted, usually causes considerable psychological shock and physical complications, particularly when the operation is performed at an age when the girl is fully aware of what is being done to her. Table 4 illustrates the complications experienced by the women interviewed as a result of infibulation. Nevertheless, one can observe in this Table that, in spite of the pain, suffering and dangers involved, the majority of women still believed that circumcision was essential and were willing for their daughters to undergo the operation in one form or another.

Table 4[2]
Willingness to Circumcise Daughter According to Post-circumcision Experience

	Total	*Willing to Circumcise*		*Not Willing*	*Cannot Decide*
		Sunna	*Infibulation*		
Post-circumcision experience:					
Experienced significant complications	40	16	11	11	2
Experienced minor or no post-circumcision complication, fear or pain	30	16	3	9	2
Total	*70*	*32*	*14*	*20*	*4*
Percentage	*100%*	*45%*	*20%*	*29%*	*6%*

Marriage and Sexual Experience
The study shows that out of the 60 women who had been married at least once,[3] 36 said that they were anxious and frightened during the first weeks of marriage due to the effects of infibulation

complications, 20 stated that they had mixed feelings of happiness and worry, while 4 could not remember how they felt.

Twenty-five of the married respondents reported that they enjoy intercourse with their husbands, while 30 said that they do not, 5 could not explain how or what they feel during intercourse. The reasons given by the 30 women who did not enjoy sexual relations with their husbands were: lack of sexual satisfaction, 17% (10); dislike of the sexual act, 10% (6); due to feelings of pain during intercourse, 8% (5); fear of pregnancy, 10% (6); a feeling of shyness about the sexual act, 5% (3).

This question on sexual experience was the most difficult part of the interview, as Somali women are always shy, reserved and not ready to give a frank answer on issues concerning sex, especially the younger ones and most of the middle class women. But, a woman from the same society myself, who had been similarly victimized by infibulation, the women were more relaxed and willing to answer me genuinely. I am thus confident that to a great extent, the respondents' real feelings about their sexual life have been explored.

Regarding the sexual experience with infibulated women of the men in the sample, out of 32 married men (including the divorced and widowed) 25 reported that they enjoyed intercourse with their wives, whereas 7 said that they enjoyed it only partially.

The response of the men when questioned about the sexual feelings of infibulated women was as follows: of the 32 married men, 12 reported that their wives enjoy sex with them, 6 that their wives hated it, and 14 reported they did not know whether or not their wives enjoyed it.

The opinion and views of the 40 men respondents about the differences between infibulated and uncircumcised women in respect of sexual intercourse were: 12 stated that they enjoyed intercourse with non-circumcised female partners, because these seem to share with them the desire, the act and the pleasure; 14 reported that they found no difference, and 14 stated that they had not experienced intercourse with uncircumcised women.

This shows us that 57% of the men are at least *aware* that women do have feelings related to sex, whilst 44% are totally unconcerned about women's feelings (even those who do find any difference between circumcised and uncircumcised women) but only 58% (with infibulated women) and 30% (with uncircumcised women) were able to state that the women also experienced pleasure in sexual intercourse.

Concerning the male respondents' knowledge about the health hazards of circumcision 17 admitted that the practice has ill effects on women during menstruation and childbirth; 11 stated that they were not sure, while 12 pleaded ignorance about the effects of the practice. This ignorance and non-concern is also reflected in their response regarding women's health in general.

Attitudes Towards Uncircumcised Women

Public opinion about the circumcision of women is of great significance within the society and does encourage perpetuation of the practice. Men require infibulated wives and since a girl has no other choice in life but to marry, she must undergo the operation.

The respondents perception of society's attitudes towards uncircumcised females was almost similar in both sexes; these are summarized as follows:

> Society would not accept them because people would consider them loose and oversexed and would question their sexual morals and fidelity. (40 women and 25 men).
> The society would not accept them because people would regard them as unpurified Muslims. (18 women and 7 men).
> Uncircumcised females are not accepted by the society because people would look at them as a shame to the Somali culture and traditions. (12 women and 8 men).

Attitudes Towards the Circumcision of Women

We have already discussed the women in the sample who suffered complications resulting from infibulation and who, yet, were still willing for their daughters to be circumcised. Table 5 gives a clearer picture of those who desired that their daughters are circumcised, those who did not, and those who were unable to make up their mind, together with some details of their background, including marital and occupational status.

From these responses — even though a very small sample was involved — one can notice that among the women, wage employment, private business and education had made little change in their attitudes towards the circumcision of their daughters. For example, 4 out of 7 students intended that their daughters would be circumcised, while the remaining 3 rejected it.

Regarding the men's opinion, about 20 of those interviewed were in favour of circumcision for their daughters; 14 said they prescribe the Sunna form and 6 preferred infibulation. Nevertheless, it is most encouraging to find that of the men sampled, 17 stated that they would not favour any form of circumcision for their daughters. 3 of the men made no decision.

The study does show that wage employment and educational status both had some effects on the men's answers (see Table 5). Perhaps this is because they do not feel any responsibility for the future of their daughters and can afford to be more liberal regarding the practice — at least in theory. This may explain the difference between the answers of men and women in this regard.

Most women considered the practice a prerequisite for marriage and, therefore, that they should follow the general custom, otherwise no man would marry their daughters. Many respondents of both sexes were convinced that female circumcision is a religious obligation and considered it necessary, which is why the majority of them preferred the Sunna type, while those who preferred infibulation always stated as their reason, 'in order to *preserve our tradition and cultural customs*'.

A significant number, 42 women and 23 men of the total respondents were of the opinion that the custom should be abolished. In this connection, there is an obvious contradiction with the responses of the sample on circumcision of their daughters: the majority stated their willingness to do so under the present social obligations.

Therefore, it seems that everybody is reluctant to break through the established institution and tradition connected with this custom and no one dares to be the first to abandon it.

Education and so-called 'modernization'[4] have not had much effect on Somalia, and in this respect circumcision and infibulation continue in the rural as well as in the 'modern' areas. All that has changed in cities and towns is access to medical facilities such as clean instruments, anaesthesia, catgut thread and the trained midwives to perform the operation.[5]

Many younger couples have chosen the Sunna type circumcision for their daughters, but do not have the guts to totally abandon circumcision of women.

Tables 6 and 7 illustrate the response to the question of abolition or continuation of the practice according to sex, age and educational levels, in addition to revealing again that there is a majority preference to discontinue the practice. We learn from these Tables that to a certain extent both education and age affect attitudes towards the custom. As shown from the Tables, the study reveals that more of those with education and in the lower age

Table 5
Marital Status : Occupation : Desire to Circumcise Daughters. Sample 110: 70 Women and 40 Men

	Wage Employment			*Housewives and Non-Waged Males**			*Business Women/ Men*			*Students*			*Total*	
Marital Status	*Yes*	*No*	*?*	*Yes*	*No*	*?*	*Yes*	*No*	*?*	*Yes*	*No*	*?*	*No.*	*%*
Women:														
Married	15	7	0	12	1	0	2	1	0	3	2	0	*43*	*62*
Divorced	4	2	1	2	1	1	1	0	0	0	0	0	*12*	*17*
Widowed	1	1	0	1	0	0	2	0	0	0	0	0	*5*	*7*
Single	2	2	0	0	0	0	0	3	2	1	0	0	*10*	*14*
Total	22	12	1	15	2	1	5	4	2	4	2	0	*70*	*100*
%	31	17	2	21	3	1	7	6	3	6	3	0	*100*	
Men:														
Married	5	6	0	4	0	0	4	3	1	0	1	0	*24*	*60*
Divorced	1	0	0	1	0	1	1	0	0	0	0	0	*4*	*10*
Widowed	1	0	0	1	0	0	0	1	1	0	0	0	*4*	*10*
Single	0	2	0	0	1	0	0	0	0	2	3	0	*8*	*20*
Total	7	8	0	6	1	1	5	4	2	2	4	0	*40*	*100*
%	17.5	20	0	15	2.5	2.5	12.5	10	5	5	10	0	*100*	

The % is calculated to the nearest whole number and is based on the sample of each group (70 women and 40 men).
* Non-waged males are the nomads, religious men and other men who have no specific wage-employment.
Key: Yes : Desire to circumcise daughters. No : No desire to circumcise daughters. ? : Cannot decide.

groups are in favour of abolishing the custom, at least theoretically.

Reasons given to support the continuation of the practice and reasons given for the motivations of female circumcision operations were almost similar and can be summarized by the following percentages as a proportion of the total sample:

	Women	*Men*
Protection of virginity	9	5
Control of sexual desire	5	4
A tradition/Somali custom	4	2
A religious obligation	3	2
For hygienic purposes	2	1

Those who opposed continuation of the practice gave a number of interesting reasons. Several women indicated that the practice degrades their status as women, therefore it is against their fundamental human rights. Some stated that it is a useless practice — brutal, painful, harmful and serving no purpose except to torture women and deprive them of a natural sense created by God. Other women pointed out as a means to ensure and protect virginity, it was futile, as the scar can be opened and sewn back again. If it is meant to reduce sexual desire, it neither does that nor reduces temptation. The large number of prostitutes in Somalia indicates that infibulation does not prevent immorality. If it is a tradition and custom, they argued, there were many traditional beliefs which were found to be useless and harmful and had been abolished. Why is society unable to do the same with this practice? Many of them emphasized the physical health complications resulting from the practice, at every stage of the women's life cycle. Some mentioned that it has many social and psychological effects which can cause disharmony in marital relationships. A number of them believed that it was responsible for absence of sexual satisfaction. Others referred to coitus as a painful and frightening affair. Some expressed the opinion that the operation is likely to cause infertility, and referred to it as a primitive, cruel and a criminally inhuman act.

Many women pointed out that it is an ordeal for women which has no religious purpose, nor hygienic merits and should be abandoned immediately. Exceptionally, only one had pointed out that the practice was based on material motives which aimed at making the girl more attractive as a virgin in the marriage market and for the father to get more bride-price; she concluded that women should fight against this dehumanization and exploitation.

Among the men, the main reasons they offer for abolishing the custom were: it serves no purpose; it has ill effects on health; it lessens sexual desire (enjoyment) for women; it is based upon male chauvinism.

None of the sample interviewed had any real idea about the origins of the custom and its penetration into Somalia: out of 70 women, 76% (53) and 50% (20) of the men, had no idea at all of its origins and its spread in Somalia. 20% (14) women and 37% (15) men assumed that it came to Somalia through the Ancient Egyptians; 4% (3) women and 7% (3) men mentioned that it was an Islamic influence and came with the spread of Islam. 5% (2) men suggested that it arose from Cushitic culture, which had spread to Somalia from neighbouring African countries to the south of Somalia.

Table 6
Continue/Discontinue Circumcision: Attitudes According to Educational Level (Figures are for men and women combined)

Educational Level	*Continue*	*Discontinue*	*Undecided*	*Total*
Higher	8	32	4	44
Secondary	4	12	2	18
Intermediate	5	8	2	15
Elementary	4	4	—	8
No Formal	15	10	—	25
Total	*36*	*66*	*8*	*110*

Table 7
Continue/Discontinue: Attitudes According to Age (Figures for men and women combined)

Age Group	*Continue*	*Discontinue*	*Undecided*	*Total*
20–30	11	29	2	42
31–40	10	22	3	35
41-50	8	11	3	22
51-60	8	3	—	11
Total	*47*	*65*	*8*	*110*

Comments and Conclusions

Despite the limitations of this study in terms of the size of the sample, and the difficulties we faced in persuading some of the women into disclosing their personal experience of circumcision, the study indicates that the practice has spread to all classes and sections of the people. And even in the absence of statistical evidence, one can fairly conclusively state that almost everyone in Somalia follows this custom. It is a significant fact that even educated men and women afford credence to the unconfirmed religious doctrine and false beliefs. Hence, education had no great influence on the attitudes towards the custom.

As previously stated the proportion of those in the sample who were against the custom were 60% of the women, and 58% of the men. The difference in the percentages between those against and those in favour of the practice is statistically significant. It is interesting to note that the majority of those who were in favour of the continuation of female circumcision, were married and over the age of 30. Most of them had either no formal schooling or had attained lower educational levels. Among those in favour, however, were several with university or secondary education; they mostly recommended the continuation of Sunna, instead of Pharaonic circumcision, because they believe it is a tradition and has religious significance.

The practice seems to persist among all groups of women in society, both in lower and middle class categories. The study showed that the majority of women were ignorant about sex education and have inaccurate ideas about their sexual and social selves, which is the major factor that perpetuates this custom.

Although the majority of women respondents talked of the adverse effects of circumcision on their sexual desire, it cannot be safely concluded from their limited personal experiences that this is so. There is insufficient accurate data on the sexual experiences of mutilated women, but research conducted on that aspect such as by Karim, Ammar and Shandall, though minimal, found that circumcision does not necessarily reduce the sexual *desire* of the woman but does affect her capacity for sexual *pleasure*. Many experts agree that the majority of mutilated women (depending on the degree of mutilation) cannot possibly enjoy intercourse if their clitoris is removed. There is no physical possibility for a vaginal orgasm because there are no nerve ends in the vagina; therefore, if the clitoris is destroyed, women have no potentiality for experiencing orgasm.

Clinically, Karim and Ammar concluded from the results of their study of 651 circumcised women that though female circumcision '. . . does not decrease sex desire, which has a psychological more than a local background, it has a definite effect on orgasm.' [Karim and Ammar, 1965: 35].

To this effect, my study showed correlation between infibulation and sexual frustration, and this result, especially from the findings with regard to the women, seems to be acceptable in view of the complexity and consequences of Pharaonic circumcision.

In general, community attitudes, based on the findings of this study, seem to concur with the view that *circumcision of women* leads to physical and psychological complications and notably causes frigidity and sexual frustration of females.

Although the study has shown that even with educational progress, circumcision did not decline in Somalia, on the other hand, it is encouraging to find among the groups interviewed, both women and men, that the majority indicated that they were in favour of the abolition of the practice.

But it is one thing to say to a researcher that they oppose a much criticized custom, and it is another whether they are really willing to abandon it. Here, again, we find evidence of the contradiction between men's stated opinion and their readiness to have their daughters circumcised. This also seems to be confirmed by two of the case histories (see Case Story II Ardo and also Case Story III Sahra), where the mothers were reluctant to infibulate their daughters but fathers were insisting on the practice.

In the light of these observations, we can say that the economic importance of the practice (bride-price and related benefits) are still factors upon which the practice is based. The abolition of the custom would have a direct effect on bride-price as well as the control of men over women. Therefore, it is obvious that the men may not like this consequence because it is they who profit from the practice in one way or another, whether it is in the form of status and honour or whether it is in material benefits.

Future Outlook

The study did confirm the general impression that there is a growing feeling against this ancient custom in Somalia. If this is the case, we are confident that the practice will disappear when there is a greater awareness, more education for women, teaching them about sex and giving them more knowledge about their *bodies.*

Obviously to carry out a successful campaign against this practice is difficult and will take a long time; it is still a matter riddled with numerous emotionally charged beliefs and cultural taboos as the results of this study showed. Attempts to abolish the custom, therefore, should be made by way of, for example, educational and legal measures. Concerted efforts should be directed to dissemination to the community at large of accurate knowledge regarding the religious, social and psychological aspects, and the medical complications consequent upon the circumcision of women. The incidence of the wide range of abnormalities, such as keloids, cysts, calculi, fistulae, etc., with which the public are not familiar, should be exposed, as well as the damage done to women's sexuality. That these deformities and others are the result of circumcising women should be made clear.

The social and political scene in Somalia today seems conducive for combating and abolishing this practice. However, concerted effort and commitment is needed to launch campaigns that could convince the people and help to change the future outlook of the community towards women's sexuality.

Notes

1. The second or third operations are usually done when the first operation is not up to the set traditional standard, i.e., the opening left for urine and menstruation flow is not small enough.
2. Complications arising from both Sunna and infibulation amongst women interviewed for Table 4. Of those willing to circumcise their daughters: Urine Retention (8); Haemorrhage (8); Infection (3); Injury (2). Of those unwilling the figures were (4); (1); (3); (3) respectively. For those undecided, one suffered haemorrhage and one injury.
3. That means not only those who were still married but also those who were divorced and widowed.
4. It shows what 'modernization' means without change in social relationships.
5. In recent years, male nurses seem to be replacing both the traditional and trained midwives and are largely in charge of the operations in the urban areas. The number of male medical personnel performing these operations in their private dispensary clinics is relatively rising.

5. Conclusions and Recommendations

Conclusions

The subject of infibulation is central to the traditional world in Somalia; it is a socio-cultural symbol for nomadic pastoralists, agricultural communities, urban dwellers and educated elites.

The realities of their life are effectively concealed from women. This was perhaps the only tactical method possible to persuade women to support patriarchal institutions and cultural practices. Their exclusion from education and training, and other opportunities to earn an independent living prevents them developing their own capacities, except in the realm of housework and motherhood.

It is believed by some that women are the most backward elements in any society, and the most adamant in their resistance to change; but such allegations overlook the facts, and ignore the social processes whereby women are deprived from infancy, the development of their potential frustrated and their freedom of choice and opportunity curtailed.

Men will say the women perpetuate genital mutilation; that it is they who are most reluctant to change. But in Somalia, no man would marry a girl who had not been infibulated and marriage is seen as the only possible life for a woman. The practice continues not because women or men favour it but because of the overt pressure of society.

The main questions I have raised are how the notion of controlling women's sexuality arose and why has it been perpetuated? Quite clearly there is no single, simple answer to either question, a multiplicity and diversity of factors have developed as societies have moved from stage to stage. Perhaps the origin of the practice lies in the allegedly magical powers of women, (see chapter 2) and, because this power was perceived as an integral part of their sex, what more logical than to 'steal' this power by rendering women as near sexless as possible?

We can only speculate on this, but what is revealed is the paradox of women's power and influence — even dominance — *within the family*, and men's annexation of the dominant role *in society*. It seems that the greater this influence, the more dependent are men upon women, the greater the need to demonstrate their dominance. Whilst women are valued as the 'power behind the throne' only the man may be seen to occupy it! Furthermore, it seems that there is a tacit acceptance of this division of influence in all societies, and even that if challenged, a fear that the fabric of society itself may in some cases be destroyed.

I have indicated the importance of the overall, wider economic factor, but there is, within this, the narrower but no less important economic implication that men — under the compulsion to provide gifts, feasts, bride-wealth as well as maintain their wives in a fitting fashion — are just as much victims of the mores of society as are women.

Religious teachings also, upon which society bases its ethical code, have been manipulated to demonstrate that men have a sacred as well as a secular right to dominate — and even mutilate women — for their own 'good'!

A further and perhaps contemporary factor is that of conformity. There is a very strong impression that both men and women would willingly see, specifically, the practices of circumcision and infibulation abolished. But by whom? Who will make the first move? If our daughters are not traditionally mutilated who will marry them? And if no one marries them what happens to our society? Seemingly it is a vicious circle.

Whilst pointing to men as initiating and perpetuating these particular practices in order to maintain their dominance and neutralize what they see as the threat of women, we must not adopt a negative 'anti-men' attitude. The object is not that women should become dominant and men oppressed, a continuation of the 'war', but rather that men and women both as victims in one way or another of an outmoded practice must work together to change society for their mutual liberation from these archaic and pointless practices.

To change such a deeply rooted custom is difficult; *but it must and can be done.* Many similar customs have been changed; burying baby girls by Arabs in the pre-Islamic period; binding the feet of Chinese women; the burning of widows (suttee) in India;

burning of 'witches' in Europe, have all been abandoned. Genital mutilation of women in Africa must also be abandoned. There is no evidence of any kind — medical, social or religious — that such a practice serves any useful or beneficial purpose — either for women or men.

Women all over the world have begun to speak up for themselves and women's movements for their human rights and equality are gaining recognition. Fundamental changes in human attitudes can be created that are no longer dominated by fear between the sexes, but with respect and mutual understanding of each other's needs. Unless such changes are achieved, no nation can lay claim to freedom and progress.

Recommendations

The recommendations that follow are seen as initiating practical steps toward the rapid abolition of the circumcision and infibulation of women.

Government Action

1) To establish a national policy aimed at combating female circumcision.
2) To formulate a legislation necessary to forbid female circumcision throughout the country, both in the urban and rural sectors.
3) To form a national commission composed of the various ministries and agencies that are concerned with the abolition of the practice, such as the Somali Women's Organization, the Ministries of: Education, Health, Religious Affairs, Rural Development, Labour and Social Affairs, Information, The National University and other concerned bodies.

National Campaign

1) Organization of a national campaign to mobilize and arouse the consciousness of the public towards the injuriousness and uselessness of the practice; to include: Women's organizations, teachers and students, doctors, nurses, midwives and other para-medical staff, etc.
2) Encourage religious leaders to participate and pronounce on the true teachings of Islam in connection with this practice, using the mass media, in mosques and other public religious gatherings.
3) Women's organizations to take up the issue as priority in their

struggle for change, and educate women about the health hazards of the practice. They should be made aware of the real reasons behind the custom and be encouraged to oppose and eliminate the practice.
4) Trade unions, youth organizations and co-operatives to inform and educate their members about the harmful effects and the correct religious attitude toward the practice.
5) Ministry of Health to include in the Medical Faculties and Nursing Schools, appropriate courses and programmes to impart knowledge of the effects of female circumcision.
6) Efforts must be exerted to make doctors and other medical staff, as well as volunteers working in both health and social welfare sectors, aware of the facts surrounding the custom of female circumcision.
7) Both the Ministry of Health and the Women's Organization to work towards convincing traditional midwives to support them in eliminating this practice, and creating other incentives for them to enable them to earn their living.
8) Ministry of Education to include in the school's curricula the knowledge of the damage caused by female mutilation during physiology, hygiene and health education instruction.
9) To educate the public about the true facts of female circumcision and what has been scientifically proved regarding the harmful social, physical and psychological effects of the practice; information to be offered to individuals as well as to agencies and organizations, through the mass media, radio, newspapers, magazines, leaflets and pamphlets.
10) To include in the programmes of political orientation centres and mother and child health centres, factual information on the damaging effects of the genital mutilation of women.
11) To plan seminars, talks, debates and nationwide conferences of the party, social organizations and university students.

To implement these recommendations will require a massive expenditure of both time and effort on the part of the Somali Government. This entails a campaign which combines agitation for the basic and unquestionable rights of women to control their own bodies, and also to emphasize the pressing need for a developing country to have all of its citizens as fully functioning and productive members of society.

Appendix 1: Three Case Studies

Fadumo

Fadumo, a 45 year old widow with four children has been working as a cleaner in one of the government agencies. Fadumo has no formal education. Both her parents were nomads and she was born and bred in the rural areas. She settled in the town after her husband died 10 years ago. She was married at the age of 14 to a nomad and had six children, four of whom are still living, two daughters and two sons.

When asked if she still remembered the circumcision operation, she retorted: 'How can I forget such an ordeal? I remember everything as if it happened yesterday.'

Asked to give the details, she said, 'Circumcision is a common practice for Somali girls and I was expecting it when it was my turn. Little girls always look forward to this operation since they learn about it early in life.' She went on, 'I knew about the event two days earlier and was feeling happy and excited until the eve of the operation when I felt worried and could not sleep well the whole night.

'It was an early, cool morning that the circumcision took place. I was the first one to be circumcised among the three [Fadumo was circumcised with 2 older girls of her family] because I was the youngest and my mother did not want me to see what would happen to the other girls. Girls are not supposed to be cowards according to the nomadic custom and should tolerate the pain but unfortunately I could not stand the severe pain of the circumcision. I screamed when the woman performed the operation and cut my clitoris and ran away bleeding before she could sew me with the thorns.[1] My mother and the midwife caught me and all the women around held me tight and pressed me down until the woman operator finished sewing me up.'

When asked what kind of instruments had been used for the cutting and sewing of the operation, she recalled that a sharp knife was used for cutting and as customary, thorns were used for joining up the two sides of the wound. Also she reported that certain traditional herbs were used for the treatment of the wound. In the rural areas, she said: 'They always dig a hole in the ground, light a fire and burn certain herbs and circumcised girls sit over it. It helps the wound become dry and also its aromatic smell kills the unpleasant odour of urine and blood.'

Fadumo recalled that she bled for three days, the bleeding was stopping and starting until her mother decided to take her to the nearest village clinic (Out-patient clinic). She said, 'My mother remained with me in that village for about two weeks, where we stayed with some relatives until I was able to go back to the nomadic area with my mother. My mother was nursing me all the time and the village male nurse came to check on me every second day. I was fed with special foods during the time I was sick, in order to make up for my lost blood. I was given liver, milk and meat.'

Fadumo was then asked about her experiences during her wedding. She replied: 'I was afraid and worried about everything because I was young, and my father made all the arrangements for my marriage to a man 20 years older than myself. Later I discovered that he had given a large number of camels to my family as a bride-price.'

'I suffered a lot during my wedding time. The custom in my region was, and still is, that the man defibulates his bride. My husband used a knife to cut the infibulation and when I tried to run away and struggled, he accidentally cut the sides of my legs and the whole area was messed up with blood. I lost a lot of blood and then developed a constant fever and my vagina became swollen. I was terribly sick when my mother came and took me home. After that I was taken to Galkaayo Hospital (the nearest town to us) where I stayed for a week.

'My family decided to keep me with them until I regained my strength and grew mature enough for the marriage burden and responsibilities. I stayed with them for two complete years before they took me back to my husband.

'After I stayed with my husband for two nights of painful intercourse and fear, I decided to run away and I went back to my family. I did not listen to all their persuasions and did not go back. This time also I was separated from my husband for about another two years. At the age of 18 years, I was returned to my husband, still against my will. When I stayed there for a few weeks, tolerating my dislike of the man and his sexual desires, for the sake of pleasing my family, I discovered that I was pregnant and I stayed with him and stopped running away.'

Fadumo was asked if she enjoyed her sexual relations with her husband after that. She replied with obvious disgust: 'I do not remember ever enjoying such a relationship. Even when the pain and difficult times were over, I used to feel terribly frightened. I always used to submit to it out of duty and just to have children.'

Fadumo said that each pregnancy resulted in prolonged labour, sometimes for two days, and each time she suffered some infection. All her children were born at home in the rural areas with the assistance of a traditional midwife.

Both Fadumo's daughters were circumcised and infibulated at the age of eight and nine years. She said, 'Although I had suffered so much because of circumcision, it is a traditional custom and I had to have it done.'

Fadumo, when she was asked why women are circumcised said that it is shameful not to be circumcised and men derive pleasure only from circumcised women. 'Of course, no woman can marry without circumcision in our country. I heard only recently that non-Muslim women are not circumcised, but I have not heard of any people in Somalia who do not circumcise their daughters.'

Fadumo was asked if she thought the practice should be abolished. She said that if religious and government leaders thought that girls should not be circumcised, she would be the first one to support them because of her own experiences of its serious, harmful effects. 'Women' she said 'suffer a lot from this operation, from childhood until their old age. Girls can hardly urinate when they are virgins because they are tightly sewn up. They have the same problem with their monthly periods,' she added.

Fadumo related how '. . . it used to take us hours to finish our morning urine. We girls used to get up very early, before the rest of the family were awake, and go to the forest in groups but it was always hard to get rid of all the urine because it came in drops and never finished properly. We envied our mothers and grandmothers when they went to urinate in the forest in their turn and came back quickly. We looked forward to the day when we could do this, and when menstruation would come and finish without pain and difficulty. Marriage was a new problem and a solution at the same time.'

2. Ardo

Ardo is a 32 year old graduate of an intermediate school with secretarial training and works as a typist in one of the government ministries. She was born and raised in Mogadiscio; her father was a religious leader and her mother was a housewife with no formal schooling. Ardo was circumcised and infibulated at the age of seven along with several other girls.

When asked how she was circumcised and on whose decision Ardo replied: 'I was the one who initiated my circumcision when I saw some of my friends in the neighbourhood were being circumcised. My mother was delighted to see my eagerness and agreed to include me with the group. I was then circumcised at the same time as these girls.

'I was excited and happy when my mother agreed, but when I saw the woman operator and her razor blade, I felt frightened. When it was my turn I was already trembling but forced myself to sit down so that my mother would not see that I was afraid. When the women there held me tight and the midwife parted my legs, I was full of fear and when she started the cutting, I screamed loudly and fought to free myself. One of the women filled my mouth with cloth, another one closed my eyes and they kept me tight and suffocated me with their bosoms until I nearly ran out of air. By the time the operation was over, I was exhausted and hardly breathing. My mother told me that the operator used six thorns to sew up my wound, three on each side. I did not know what was happening to me except that I was feeling severe pain. I also felt the rough, strong fingers of the woman operator.

'After the operation, I stayed in bed for two days without moving, as I was afraid to do so. I refused to urinate as well, but even when I tried to on the second day, I could not as it was so painful. My bladder was so full and hard and I was crying.

'Because of this my father decided that I should be taken to the hospital. When the doctor examined me, he took the thorns out of the wound and then helped me to urinate. After all the urine was out I felt relieved of my pain.

'After two days, my mother insisted that I should be sewn again and called another midwife. I cried and resisted but they were stronger than I was and the midwife sewed me up again. This time I felt pain but it was not as painful as the cutting of the clitoris.

'On the fourth day of my second operation, the midwife came and took out the thorns. My legs were tied up for several days and

I was walking with the support of a stick for another few days. It took me about two weeks to resume any other activities. My mother nursed me, cleaned the wound, applied herbs, burned small incense under my legs and used to feed me with traditional 'mug mad' (dried Somali meat) porridge and milk.

'Seven years after I found that I had something hard and big on the scar of the infibulation.[2] It was like a small ball. I went to see a doctor. He told me it was nothing serious and was a common complaint with infibulation which could be remedied by a minor operation. I was admitted to hospital, underwent the operation from which it took me a week to recover.'

Ardo continued to say that she knew many girls and women who suffered from circumcision and had heard of certain sad cases of young girls who bled to death as a result of the operation, particularly in the rural areas. 'You see', she said, 'people always hide such incidents.'

When Ardo was asked why she thought that women undergo these tortures, she replied, 'It is a deep rooted custom in our culture and people think it is an important operation for women because it prevents them from being over-sexed. Uncircumcised girls are not accepted among our society. As you know, infibulation is a prerequisite for marriage because no man wants to have an oversexed woman who becomes unfaithful after marriage. No family wants their daughter to have "loose" ways and bring shame to the family. Because of this, mothers make sure that their daughters are properly circumcised and infibulated.'

When Ardo was asked about her married life experience, she replied, 'Well, I got married to my first husband when I was 15 years old and I never liked that man, he was too old for me — about 40 years old. Only my father decided that I should marry him. He was always a stranger to me. At that time, nobody told me anything about marriage and how to deal with such a situation. On my wedding night there was a big ceremony and all my friends and my relatives and my husband's were present. I was given many presents and beautiful things. But it was the most terrible evening of my life.

'When I was left alone with this strange man for the first time, I felt shy and afraid at the same time and did not know what to expect from this strange man.

'The first nights of my wedding were really awful and filled with fear. The custom in Benader region is for the men to defibulate their brides with their penis. Except in very rare cases it is an insult if they use an instrument or if (as in the northern region) the midwife defibulates. Anyway, I refused to submit or cooperate with my husband. I shouted and fought with him, and bit him seriously. Five days after my wedding, the man was still not able to have intercourse with me. Then I was forced to go to the hospital where they opened my infibulation. After that I got an infection and was sick for a few days before the man forced me again.

'I was never happy with that first husband and I continued to hate him and fought with him in every sexual contact. I finally left him, and refused to go back, until he agreed to divorce me.

'With my second husband, I can say that I am happy, because he was my own choice this time. I rarely enjoy sex with him because I still have some reservations and bad memories about it.'

Ardo has two children now, a daughter and a son. She said that she will not have her daughter infibulated but she will have the Sunna circumcision for her. She said that her husband also prefers the Sunna circumcision but would not agree with her not to have her daughter circumcised.

She said, 'As long as we are Muslims, I do not know why we do not use only Sunna which will not involve the same difficulties and complications of the infibulation.'

Ardo condemns the practice of infibulation but supports the mild form of circumcision which she believes is a religious obligation.

3. Sahra

Sahra, a 35 year old mother of six children (four daughters and two sons) was a housewife with no formal education; she was, however, born and brought up in a town. Her father was a policeman and her mother a housewife with no formal schooling. Sahra married a literate civil servant who has since become a successful businessman.

She was circumcised alone at the age of seven years. She said, 'It was my aunt's decision as my mother died when I was four years old.'

Asked to tell us something about her circumcision experience, Sahra said, 'I have so much to tell as I had to undergo that horrible operation three times.

'It was an early morning when the traditional midwife came

with her instrument bag and performed the operation', Sahra continued, 'I knew I was going to be circumcised because my aunt kept telling me that it was time that I should, as I must be clean and that it would help me to grow up quickly into a fine big girl like my sister.

'I was very much afraid of the woman operator when she opened her dirty bag and produced the knife. (I was told later it was a razor blade.) I was held very firm and tight and my back was pressed back by some women friends of my aunt and some relatives. When my legs were parted the midwife started to perform the operation, I felt great pain and I screamed and fought wildly, but it was not possible to free myself. After all these years, I still remember the pain and how frightened I was. When it was over, I could hear the ululations of the women, and then they broke an egg on the wound which they said would cool down the sharp pain. They also used *melmel*[3] and other traditional herbs. In spite of this I started to bleed and they were not able to stop it until the midwife took out the thorns. Then the bleeding stopped and she put more herbs on the wound. I was left like that for four days. They did not take me to hospital but my aunt and the operator were nursing me at home. The fourth day of my first operation, the midwife came again with her knife, I was held tightly again and then reinfibulated with several thorns. I was very shocked and shivering with fear and pain.

'At the age of 12, I was told that my infibulation was not proper (i.e., not tight enough) and therefore, I had to have another operation. I was very unhappy about it, but I was told I would not be regarded as a decent girl if I was not tightly infibulated. Other girls of my age would laugh at me and gossip about me and also there would be no hope for me to marry if I was not infibulated well and according to the customary standard. It was a horrible, painful and sickening experience for me but I had to force myself to undergo it.

'That third operation was successful. This time I was very careful with my movements even when I was allowed to walk. My aunt also nursed me very carefully. I was fed with little fluids and plain white rice and porridge with very little butter for the first three days, so that I would not urinate and defecate frequently during the first few days after the operation. After the first week, circumcised girls are usually given better foods, like meat, milk etc., to help them regain their health.'

Sahra told us that menstruation was very painful, particularly before she was married. 'I used to vomit and feel terrible abdominal pain and backache but I am much relieved since I got married and especially after I had children.

'My wedding was another unpleasant period of my life', Sahra said. She continued to explain: 'On the second day of my wedding around 5 o'clock in the afternoon, the midwife came to defibulate me. Of course I knew what was going to happen to me because my married friends had told me about the sufferings and torture of the wedding night. When I saw the midwife and other women waiting for me, I pretended I was going to the bathroom, I locked myself in and refused to come out. This spoiled everything that evening and the appointment with the operator was postponed to the next day. I refused to open the door until the next morning. That day I was warned that if I refused to submit to the midwife, they would call men to defibulate me by force.[4] So after resisting for a few hours I gave up and submitted myself to the operation because I was more afraid of the men cutting me up. I had heard some cases of girls who ran away during their wedding time and then were caught and cut by strong men.'

Sahra described her wedding nights as difficult, miserable nights, full of fear, worries, sleeplessness and sometimes even physical struggle and fights with her husband to prevent frequent, painful intercourse.

Sahra said that she is happy with her husband now, but even after 15 years of marriage still hates the sexual act. She said, 'I have strange feelings about it, but I could never explain them. I do not know whether my cold feelings are due to circumcision or to other factors. I thought every woman had the same feelings, until I discussed them with a friend of mine.' Childbirth, she told us was always difficult, with much suffering before and after.

Asked if her daughters were infibulated, Sahra answered, 'I did have my two elder daughters infibulated but I will not have my youngest daughters infibulated. She said that she still regrets having had her daughters infibulated and blames this on the influence of her husband. She said, 'My husband is in favour of girls being circumcised and infibulated. I know he will not agree that our younger daughters shall not be infibulated but I will insist regardless of what happens to them in the future.'

Sahra strongly opposed the continuation of the practice, saying 'It is really a brutal practice which makes women suffer all their lives. I believe it is not a religious obligation but was just intended by men to control women's sexuality like animals. I think it is time now that women should stand together and fight against this useless old custom.'

Notes

1. Usually there is a short break between the first phase of the operation (the cutting of the clitoris) and the second phase (infibulating or sewing up the sides).
2. Such a boil or growth is called keloid. It is a very common complication related to the infibulation scar. Many infibulated women are treated for this by a minor operation if they go to hospitals, but a large number of women hide this kind of complaint.
3. *Melmel* is a sticky jellylike stuff which helps the sides of the wound to adhere.
4. The custom in the northern region of Somalia is that if the bride refuses to be defibulated by the midwife, the male friends of the bridegroom take on the role and defibulate the bride by force, as a form of punishment.

Appendix 2: Questionnaires Administered (Women and Men)

1. **Age:**
2. **Place of Birth:** **Town:** **Countryside:**
3. **Educational Background:** No formal schooling/Elementary education/Intermediate Education/Secondary Education/ Higher Education.
4. **Occupation:** Student/Housewife/Employed/Other.
5. **Fathers Education and Occupation:**
6. **Mothers Education and Occupation:**
7. **Where did you live when you were young?** Village/Town/ Interior.
8. **Are you circumcised?** Yes/No.
9. **If yes, at what age were you circumcised?**
10. **Who initiated that you should get circumcised?** Mother/ Father/Grandmother/Aunt/Other/Do not know.
11. **How was your feeling when you were getting ready to be circumcised?**
12. **Who performed the operation?** Grandmother/Traditional midwife/Trained midwife or nurse/Other/Do not know.
13. **Where did it take place?** In hospital/In your house/Under a tree/In the town/In a village/In the operators house.
14. **Were you circumcised alone or with other girls?**
15. **What type was your circumcision?** Sunna/Pharaonic/Other.
16. **Can you briefly describe how the operation was performed?** (with what instrument, who was there, how were you held, how did you feel, e.g. screamed, cried or fought, etc.).
17. **Do you remember any immediate complications that you suffered then or after the operation?** Fear/Shock/Bleeding/ Injuries/Urinary complications/Other.

18. If yes, please describe clearly what complication it was.
19. After circumcision how long did you remain in bed?
20. Who was nursing you?
21. Did you have any kind of celebration (e.g. any songs, party, gifts, etc.)?
22. Did you have any special food during that time?
23. Was your first circumcision operation successful? Yes/No.
24. How did you feel at the time of the second operation? Sad/Happy/Worried/Shocked/Other.
25. Why did they tell you to do it again?
26. Are all females in your family circumcised?
27. Do you know why girls are circumcised? Is this: Control of female sexual desire/To protect girls virginity/Hygienic purposes/Tradition/Somali custom/Religious obligation/Do not know/Other.
28. What do people say about uncircumcised girls?
29. Are you familiar with the origin of this practice and how and when it started in Somalia?
30. Did you feel pain with your monthly period (menstruation)? If yes, please state what complications you had.

Marital Status

31. Are you: Married/Single/Divorced (if so why)/Widowed.
32. Years of marriage. 33. Number of Children:
34. Did you marry more than once?
35. If yes, how many times?
36. At what age did you get married?
37. Were you afraid of marriage because you were infibulated?
38. If yes, please say why?
39. What were your feelings during your wedding night?
40. Did anyone tell you what happens to you during your wedding night?
41. Describe what happened to you during the wedding days in connection with your infibulation.
42. Did you get any complications?
43. If yes, state what complications (e.g. infection, bleeding, fear, pain, etc. and how long it continued).
44. Are you happy in your married life? Yes/No/If not, why?

45. **Do you enjoy sex with your husband?** Yes/No/Do not know.
46. **If not, why:** Because you feel pain/Lack of sexual satisfaction/ Feel shy/Hate the sexual act/Afraid to get pregnant/Other.
47. **If you have children, where did you have your deliveries?** House/Hospital/Other
48. **Who assisted in your deliveries if you had them at home?** Neighbour/Traditional midwife/Trained midwife/Other.
49. **Did you have difficult deliveries, miscarriages,** etc.
50. **Do you think circumcision has any effect on painful menstruation or childbirth?**
51. **If yes, please specify these effects?**
52. **Did you hear any women complaining of infibulation and to what extent?**
53. **Do you have any opinion of how doctors feel about this practice?** Yes/No.
54. **If yes, do you agree with their opinion?**
55. **If you have daughters did you circumcise them?** Why?
56. **If you have a daughter would you circumcise her?** Why?
57. **If yes, which type of circumcision?** Infibulation/Sunna/Other.
58. **What does your husband think about this subject?**
59. **Would he agree not to circumcise your daughter?** Yes/No/Do not know.
60. **Do you think that female circumcision should continue?** Yes/No.
61. **Please give reasons.**

1. Age: 2. Place of Birth:
3. Educational background: No formal schooling/Elementary education/Intermediate education/Secondary education/Higher education.
4. Occupation:
5. Married/Single/Widower/Divorced (why).
6. Years of marriage:
7. Number of marriages?
8. Number of children (if any)? Male/Female.
9. Number of sisters if any?
10. Are all the females in your family circumcised?
11. If you have daughters are they circumcised?
12. If you have a daughter would you circumcise her?
13. What do people say about girls who are not circumcised?
14. Would your wife agree with you if you did not circumcise your daughter?
15. Do you know why girls are circumcised? If yes, please give reasons.
16. Do you have any idea how this practice originated, and how it started in Somalia?
17. Did you hear any women complaining of circumcision complications?
18. Do you think circumcision and infibulation have any effect on menstruation or childbirth? If yes, why?
19. Do you enjoy sex with your wife? Yes/No/If not, why?
20. Does your wife enjoy sex with you? Yes/No/Do not know/Why?

21. **What does your wife think about this subject?** (sex).
22. **Did you ever have sex with uncircumcised women?** Yes/No. If yes, did you enjoy sex with her more than infibulated women?
23. **Do you think female circumcision should continue?** Yes/No. Please give reasons.

Bibliography

Abou-Zeid, A.M., (1965) Honour and Shame among the Bedouins of Egypt in Peristiany, J.G. (ed.) *Honour and Shame*. The Value of Mediterranean Society, London: Weidenfeld & Nicolson.

Abu-Shamma, A.O. et.al., (1941) 'Female Circumcision in Sudan', *Lancet*, 545.

Alfred C. Kinsey and Staff of the Institute for Sex Research, (1953) *Sexual Behaviour in the Human Female.* University of Indiana, W.B. Saunders Co., Philadelphia.

Al-Aazzaz, A., (1978) 'Current Status of Research on Women in the Arab World', *Middle Eastern Studies*, Vol.14, p.372–80.

Antoun, Richard T., (1968) 'On the Modesty of Women in Arab Muslim Villages: A Study in the Accommodation of Traditions', *American Anthropologist*, Vol.70, No.4, pp.671–97.

Assaad, Maria B., (1979) 'Female Circumcision in Egypt: Current Research and Social Implications', UNICEF.

Baashir, T.A., (1977) 'Psychological Aspects of Female Circumcision', a Paper presented to the 5th Congress of The Obstetrical and Gynaecological Society of Sudan. (Khartoum, 14–18 February).

Badri, Gasim, (1979) 'Psychosocial Aspects of Female Circumcision in the Sudan', a Paper presented in the Seminar of Traditional Practices Affecting the Health of Women and Children.

Beck, Dorothy Fabs, (1967) 'The Changing Moslem Family in the Middle East', *Marriage and Family Living*, Vol.19, No.4, pp.350–347.

Beck, Louis and Nikki Keddie, (1978) (Ed.) *Women in the Muslim World*, Harvard University Press, Cambridge, Massachusetts and London.

Benfield, Barker, (1976) *The Horrors of the Half-Known Life: Male Attitudes Toward Women and Sexuality in Nineteenth Century America*, New York, Harper and Row.

Bond, Caroline & Hermione Harris, (1975) 'Library Research on Female Circumcision'. Report from Anti-Slavery Society for the Protection of Human Rights.

Bowesman, Charles, (1960) 'Ritual Circumcision of Females', from *Surgery and Clinical Pathology in the Tropics*, Published by

Livingstone Ltd., Edinburgh and London.

Bullough, Vern L., (1976) *The Subordinate Sex: A History of Attitudes Toward Women*, University of Illinois Press.

Burton, Richard Francis, (1898) *Personal Narrative of Pilgrimage to Al Madinah and Meccah*, Vol.11, George Bell & Sons, London, pp.19-20.

Cook, Dr Robin, (1976) 'Damage to Physical Health from Pharaonic Circumcision (Infibulation) of Females: A Review of the Medical Literature', World Health Organization Regional Office for the Eastern Mediterranean.

Daly, Mary, (1975) *Ainsi soit-elle?* Paris.

Daly, Mary, (1978) *Gynaecology and Mataethics of Radical Feminism*, Beacon Press, Boston, Massachusetts.

Dualeh, Raqiya H., (1977) 'Sexual Oppression of Women in the Third World' Paper presented to the Institute of Social Studies, The Hague.

El Dareer, Asma, (1980) 'A Study on Prevalence and Epidemiology of Female Circumcision in the Sudan', Department of Community Medicine, Faculty of Medicine, University of Khartoum, Sudan.

El Suadawi, Nawal, *The Hidden Face of Eve: Women in the Arab World.*

Engels, Friedrich, (1977) *The Origin of the Family, Private Property and the State*, Translated by Alec West as published in 1942. Lawrence and Wishart, London.

Fernea, W. Elizabeth and Bezirgan Q. Basima (eds.), (1977) *Middle Eastern Muslim Women Speak*, University of Texas Press/Austin and London.

Fleming, J.B., (1960) 'Clitoridectomy: The Disastrous Downfall of Isaac Baker Brown', F.R.C.S., *Journal of Obstetrics and Gynaecology of the British Commonwealth*, Vol.67, pp.1017-34.

Frazer, J.G., (1923) *The Golden Bough*, London, p.7.

Ghalioungui, P., (1963) *Magic and Medicine Science in Ancient Egypt*, Hodder and Stoughton, London.

Ghalioungui, P. (1973) 'The House of Life Per Ankh Magic and Medicine Science in Ancient Egypt', Amsterdam, B.M. Isreal.

Hansen, H.H., (1972/73) 'Clitoridectomy: Female Circumcision in Egypt', *Folk (Kobenhaven)* Vol.1415, pp.16-26.

Hathout, H.M., (1963) 'Some Aspects of Female Circumcision: With a Case Report of a Rare Complication', *Journal of Obstetrics and Gynaecology*, Vol.79, pp.505-7.

Hayes, Rose Oldfield, (1975) 'Female Genital Mutilation, Fertility Control, Women's Roles and the Patrilineage in Modern Sudan', *American Ethnologist*, Vol.2, No.4.

Hosken, Fran P., (1979) *The Hosken Report — Genital and Sexual Mutilation of Females*, (Second Enlarged Edition), Women's International Network News.

Hosken, Fran P., (1980) 'Female Sexual Mutilations: The Facts and Proposals For Action', Women's International Network News.

Huber, A., (1966) 'Weibliche Zirkumzision und Infibulation in

Athiopia (A Survey of Female Circumcision and Infibulation in Ethiopia)', Acla Tropica, Basel, pp.87-91.

Imperalo, P. James, (1977) *African Folk Medicine: Practice and Beliefs of the Bambara and other Peoples.* York Press Inc. Baltimore, Maryland.

Ismail, Edna A., 'Female Circumcision in Somalia' Paper presented at the Institute of Social Studies, The Hague, 1977.

Karim, M. and Ammar, R., (1965) *Female Circumcision and Sexual Desire*, Ain Shamis University Press, Cairo, Egypt.

Kennedy, John G., (1970) 'Circumcision and Excision in Egyptian Nubia', *Man*, Vol.5, No.2, pp.175–91 (Ethnographic Study).

Kenyatta, Jomo, (1965) *Facing Mount Kenya*, Vintage Books, Random House, New York (First published in 1930s).

King, M.J.S., (1890), 'On the Practice of Female Circumcision and Infibulation among the Somalis and Other Nations of North-East Africa', Anthropological Society, Bombay, (ii, pp.2–6).

Laycock, H.T., (1950) 'Surgical Aspects of Female Circumcision in Somaliland', *East African Medical Journal*, Vol.27, pp.445–50.

Levy, R., (1963) *The Social Structure of Islam*, London, Cambridge University Press.

Lewis, Ian M., (1962) 'Marriage and the Family in Northern Somaliland', Kampala, *East African Institute of Social Research.*

Longo, L.D., (1964) 'Socio-cultural Practices Relating to Obstetrics and Gynaecology in a Community in West Africa' *American Journal of Obstetrics and Gynaecology*, 1964 (89) 4.

Masters and Johnson, (1966) *Human Sexual Response*, Little, Brown Co., Boston.

Meinardus, Otto, (1967) 'Mythological, Historical and Sociological Aspects of the Practice of Female Circumcision Among the Egyptians', Acta Ethnographica Academiae Scientiarum Hungaricae, (Reprint) pp.387-97.

Melly, J.M., (1935) 'Infibulation', *Lancet* (2), 1272.

Mernissi, Faduma, (1975) *Beyond the Veil, Male–Female Dynamics in Modern Muslim Society*, Schenkman Publishing Co. Inc., Cambridge, Massachusetts.

Modawi, Suliman, (1973) 'The Impact of Social and Economic Changes on Female Circumcision', Proceedings of the Third Congress of Obstetrics and Gynaecology, Khartoum. Sudan Medical Association Congress Series No.I, 1974, pp.242–54.

Montagu, Ashley, (1953) *The Natural Superiority of Women*, The Macmillan Company, New York.

Murray, J.M., (1974) 'The Kikuyu Female Circumcision Controversy, With Special Reference to the Church', University of California, Los Angeles.

Musa, I. Galaal, (1968) 'Somali Traditional Marriage', a Paper prepared for Somali Academic Studies.

Otoo, S.N.A., (1976) 'Pharaonic Circumcision in Somalia', WHO, EMRO, Unpublished Report.

Parweg, G.A., (1968) 'Islam: A Challenge to Religion', Gulberg, Lahore, Pakistan.

Pridle, E.D. et al., (1951) *Female Circumcision in the Anglo-Egyptian Sudan*, Sudan Government Publication (McC 285) S.G.1185 C.S. 500 6/51.

Remondino, P.C. (1891) *History of Circumcision from the Earliest Times to the Present*, F.A. Davis Co., Philadelphia.

Ruether, R. Rosemary (ed.), (1974) 'Religion and Sexism' *Images of Women in the Jewish and Christian Tradition*, Simon and Schuster, New York.

Sequeira, J.H., (1931) 'Female Circumcision and Infibulation', *Lancet* Vol.2, pp.1054–56.

Shaalan, Mohammed, (1979) 'Clitoris Envy: A Psychodynamic Construct Instrument in Female Circumcision', a Paper presented in the Seminar on Traditional Practices Affecting the Health of Women', Khartoum, Sudan.

Shandall, A.A.F., (1967) 'Circumcision and Infibulation of Females', *Sudan Medical Journal*, Vol.5, No.5, pp.178–212.

Share Hite, (1976) *The Hite Report*, Dell Publishing Co. Inc., New York.

Taba, A.H., (1979) 'Female Circumcision', *The Magazine of the World Health Organization*, pp.8–13.

Taoko, Jean G., (1975) 'L'Excision: Base de la Stabilite Familiale ou Rite Cruel?' in *Famille et Developpement*, Dakar, Senegal.

Verzin, J.A., (1975) 'Sequelae of Female Circumcision', *Tropical Doctor*, Vol.5, pp.163–69.

Widstrand, C.G., (1965) 'Female Infibulation', *Studia Ethnographica Uppsala*, pp.95–124.

Worsley, Allan, (1938) 'Infibulation and Female Circumcision: A Study of a Little-known Custom', *British Journal of Obstetrics and Gynaecology*, (45), pp.686–91.

Zwang, Gerard, (1977) 'Female Sexual Mutilation — Technique and Results', WHO Report.